MARXISM AND THE PARTY

The International Socialism book series (IS Books) aims to make available books that explain the theory and historical practice of working class self-emancipation from below. In so doing, we hope to rescue the main tenets of the revolutionary socialist tradition from its detractors on both the right and left. This is an urgent challenge for the left today, as we seek to rebuild this tradition in circumstances that often downplay the importance of organized revolutionaries.

By reissuing classics of the international socialist tradition, we hope to offer accessible and unique resources for today's generation of socialists.

Other titles in the International Socialism series:

Leon Trotsky and the Organizational Principles of the Revolutionary Party
Dianne Feeley, Paul Le Blanc, and Thomas Twiss,
introduction by George Breitman

Mandate of Heaven: Marx and Mao in Modern China
Nigel Harris

The Duncan Hallas Reader (forthcoming)
Edited by Ahmed Shawki

The Lost Revolution: Germany 1918 to 1923
Chris Harman

Marxism and the Party
John Molyneux

Party and Class
Tony Cliff, Duncan Hallas, Chris Harman, and Leon Trotsky

Russia: From Workers' State to State Capitalism
Anthony Arnove, Tony Cliff, Chris Harman, and Ahmed Shawki

MARXISM AND THE PARTY

JOHN MOLYNEUX

Haymarket Books
Chicago, Illinois

This edition published in 2003 and 2017 by
Haymarket Books
P.O. Box 180165
Chicago, IL 60618
773-583-7884
www.haymarketbooks.org
info@haymarketbooks.org

ISBN: 978-1-60846-572-9

Trade distribution:
In the US, Consortium Book Sales and Distribution, www.cbsd.com
In Canada, Publishers Group Canada, www.pgcbooks.ca
In the UK, Turnaround Publisher Services, www.turnaround-uk.com
All other countries, Ingram Publisher Services International,
intlsales@perseusbooks.com

This book was published with the generous support of Lannan Foundation
and Wallace Action Fund.

Cover design by Eric Kerl.

Printed in Canada by union labor.

Library of Congress Cataloging-in-Publication data is available.

10 9 8 7 6 5 4 3 2 1

Contents

Introduction

This book was written in the mid-1970s and, like any other work, bears the imprint of its times. The early 1970s in Britain were years of massive and largely successful working-class struggle: highpoints were the destruction of the Tory government's Industrial Relations Act by the dockers and engineering workers, the breaking of the wages freeze by the miners in 1972, and finally the bringing down of the Tory government of Edward Heath by the miners' strike of 1974. There were defeats, of course, but generally the picture showed a rising working-class movement.

Internationally too there were grounds for considerable optimism. The marvellous year of 1968 was still relatively fresh in our minds, with the Tet offensive in Vietnam, the dramatic May events in France, the worldwide spread of student revolt, and the black riots across the cities of America. Moreover, 1968 was followed by the Italian workers' 'hot summer' in 1969, the crushing defeat over the US in Vietnam, and the Portuguese Revolution of 1974 with its many consequences in Africa. Once again there were defeats, most notably the terrible tragedy of the Chilean coup in 1973, but overall it appeared that the world revolutionary process was gaining ground.

In particular it seemed that the forces of authentic revolutionary Marxism were at last beginning to claw themselves back from the outer fringes of political life, to which they had been consigned since the rise of Stalinism in the 1920s. In Britain the International Socialists (now the Socialist Workers Party) had transformed themselves from a tiny propaganda group of a couple of hundred people into a viable mini-party of several thousands with a small but serious base in the working class. In Europe there were a number of promising groups of a similar or larger size who, while their politics were somewhat confused (the influence of Maoism was strong), were nonetheless clearly revolutionary and had a definite orientation towards the working class. As *Marxism and the Party* put it, there was 'the emergence in various countries of sizeable organisations (not mass parties but large enough to constitute a serious beginning) with the aim of building the revolutionary party'.

The perspective underlying *Marxism and the Party* was that these trends would continue and that substantial revolutionary parties would grow and develop, not only in Britain but in a number of other countries. Unfortunately it has to be admitted that this perspective has not been realised. Overall the working-class movements in the advanced capitalist countries, and with them the forces of revolutionary socialism, are somewhat weaker than they were a decade ago.

The shift in the balance of class forces in Britain is epitomised by the contrasting fates of the miners' strikes of 1974 and 1984–5. The defeat of 1985 was the culmination and consequence of a long series of setbacks that had undermined the militancy and solidarity of the labour movement.

Underlying this process has been the fact that the onset of the long-awaited world economic crisis in 1974, and its continuation (punctuated by small revivals) up to the present day, has not produced the mass radicalisation of workers that revolutionary socialists had expected. Rather it has produced a decline into demoralisation. The long recession has exposed the bankruptcy of the reformist trade-union consciousness which dominated the workers' movement, but it has done so at a time when revolutionaries have been not nearly strong enough to constitute a serious alternative pole of attraction. Workers who would go on to the offensive and score victory after victory when they believed 'the money was there', with a certain proportion of them drawing revolutionary conclusions in the process, have become more cautious and reluctant to fight when convinced that the employer might really be about to go under or that 'the country couldn't afford it'.

These are very broad generalisations to which there have been, of course, many exceptions and countervailing tendencies. On a world scale there have been a number of magnificent struggles and some notable victories—the *Solidarność* movement in Poland, the Sandinista revolution in Nicaragua, the overthrow of the Shah of Iran and so on—but for one reason or another none has given revolutionary socialism the same international inspiration as May '68 or the defeat of the US in the Vietnam war. The result has been a lean period for the revolutionary left in which my own organisation, the SWP, has done well to maintain itself and grow a little, and in which many other would-be revolutionary parties have either shrunk, collapsed, or moved to the right.

Despite this sombre balance sheet I believe the basic ideas of *Marxism and the Party* remain relevant to the present situation. The defeats and setbacks of the past decade have been due not to the presence but to the absence of the kind of Marxist parties that I advocate in this book. These defeats made it harder to build such parties, but they have also confirmed the necessity of continuing the attempt. Moreover the attempt remains practical, for the defeats, though serious, have generally been partial rather than total. The workers' movement has been weakened, indeed, but not dismantled and crushed as it was, for example, in those European countries which succumbed to fascism between the two world wars or, for that matter, in the USSR under Stalin. Thus there continue to be many workers' struggles to which revolutionaries can relate and a small but growing minority of workers who not only want to fight, but also want explanations for past failures and are looking for ideas and strategies that can lead to victory in the future.

The need for a revolutionary party is posed concretely in Britain by the recent evolution of the Labour Party. The decline of the left current that had formed around Tony Benn since its heyday in 1982 and the rightward shift of the party under the leadership of Neil Kinnock confronts all genuine socialists in the Labour Party with the necessity to make a clean break with reformism. It is now clear that a future Labour government under Neil Kinnock (or a coalition government of Labour and the Social Democratic Party) will be a disaster for the working class, probably worse than the disastrous Wilson-Callaghan administration of the late-1970s, unless it faces massive resistance from below. At the centre of such resistance, giving it coherence and perspective, must be a revolutionary Marxist party.

Consequently, if I had time to rewrite or revise *Marxism and the Party* today (which I do not) the main lines of the argument and its principal conclusions would remain unchanged. It is still very much the case, as I wrote then, that the building of revolutionary parties and their international unification is now the principal and most urgent strategic task facing revolutionary socialists throughout the world. Unless this is achieved, the working class will be unable to resolve in its favour the crisis of capitalism which grows more acute by the day!

However there would, of course, be certain changes of emphasis. The most significant of these concerns the assessment of Gramsci. I still consider Gramsci a great revolutionary Marxist who had many important insights, but writing today I would offer a less inflated assessment of his contribution to the theory of the party. At the same time I would give more space to a strong defence of Gramsci against the Eurocommunist and academic Marxist misinterpretation that he was a reformist and prophet of the Popular Front and the 'Broad Democratic Alliance'.

These points are connected, for it is now clear to me that although Gramsci was a revolutionary who believed in the necessity of armed insurrection, *soviets* and the smashing of the capitalist state, many of his formulations—about the 'war of position' replacing the 'war of manoeuvre', the relationship between the state and civil society, and the differences between Russia and Western Europe—were imprecise and confused and thus opened the door to a reformist interpretation which Gramsci himself would have repudiated. As it stands, my chapter on Gramsci should be read in conjunction with Chris Harman's pamphlet *Gramsci versus Reformism* (London 1983) which supplies the necessary corrective.

In addition I would also devote more space to the conception of party and class embodied in Trotsky's strategic writings of 1928–37, in other words his critique of the Stalinist 'third period' ultra-leftism which divided the working class in the face of Hitler, and of the subsequent opportunism of the Popular Front period. These writings have proved extremely relevant and useful in recent years and remain so today. On the one hand they form the essential theoretical backdrop to the struggle against the revival of Nazism, which has manifested itself in Britain in the second half of the 1970s and which is going on in France today. On the other hand they are a key point of departure for Marxist criticism of the current strategy of Eurocommunism and of many other left and not-so-left reformists. The reader who wishes to follow up this question can easily do so in Duncan Hallas's *Trotsky's Marxism* (Chicago, 2003).

One thing, however, has not changed at all in the past decade. That is the urgent necessity of overthrowing capitalism if humanity, led by the working class, is to move forward from under the shadow of the nuclear mushroom cloud. If this book can contribute to this process in any way then it will serve its purpose.

Special thanks are due to Tony Cliff for his many valuable criticisms and suggestions and for his work as editor, to Anita Bromley for typing large sections of the manuscript, and to Jill, Sara and Jack for putting up with so many spoiled holidays.

John Molyneux
September 1985

1.

Karl Marx: Class and party

1. The class foundation

The foundation of all marxist approaches to the analysis of political parties is Marx's theory of class struggle. For marxists the basic explanation for the existence of different and competing political parties is to be found in the economic structure of society. Political parties come into being, attract support and continue to function primarily as the representatives of class interests.

Naturally this idea, as is the case with many marxist principles, becomes a piece of nonsense if it is understood crudely and dogmatically. The thesis that political parties represent class interests does not mean that they necessarily do so in a straightforward one-to-one relationship. It does not mean that at all times one party represents the interests of one class; or that the interests of a class, in the historical sense, can be formulated simply in terms of immediate economic gain; or that the actions of every party can be explained merely by reference to the class on which it is based. In fact history provides numerous examples of every kind of class/party combination: of parties that begin by representing the interests of one class, but end up by serving the interests of another; of parties that attempt to serve the interests of two or even three classes at once; of parties that serve a section of a class against the interests of the class as a whole; of two or three small parties competing to become the undisputed representative of the same class, and so on.

Thus in Britain today we have three major political parties:

the Tory Party, which is primarily the party of the big capitalists but is voted for by many workers and actively supported by large sections of the petty bourgeoisie;

the Labour Party, which is based in the organisations of the working class and relies mainly on workers for its votes, but which has a middle-class leadership which accepts the continuance of the capitalist system, and is therefore frequently forced to act against the interests of its working-class base;

the Liberal Party, which is basically a petty-bourgeois party, supported by a few larger capitalists and drawing some of its votes from the working class.

None of these examples refute the marxist thesis. Rather they confirm it, for all that is maintained is that the fundamental starting point for the analysis of political parties, as with politics in general, must be the class structure of the society concerned. The numerous complexities we have referred to arise from the fact that classes in society do not simply stand side by side with each other, but one on top of the other in a state of permanent and dynamic conflict, and that political parties play a major role in that conflict. A particular configuration of political parties reflects the relative stages of development reached by the different classes and the degree of hegemony attained by one class over the others. Thus when dealing with marxist theories of the party, and above all where Marx himself was concerned, one is concerned not with a narrow and separate theory of organisation, but always with the relationship between party and class. Parties are moments in the development of classes.

Marx wished to reveal the driving forces of history in order to facilitate the making of history. Thus for Marx classes are not simply static entities, but social groups which come into being through historical processes and pass through various stages of growth and maturity. Above all, classes define themselves through conflict. 'Individuals form a class only insofar as they are engaged in a common struggle with another class.'[1] In the course of the struggle classes acquire (or lose) cohesion, organisation, confidence and consciousness. Political parties are weapons in the struggle between classes.

In Marx's analysis of capitalism 'society as a whole is more and more splitting up into two great hostile camps, into two great classes directly facing each other: bourgeoisie and proletariat'.[2] It was not that Marx believed that the categories of bourgeois and proletarian covered everyone in capitalist society—to have asserted such as an empirical fact in 1847 would have been absurd. Rather, his contention was that the conflict between bougeoisie and proletariat is inherent in and fundamental to the capitalist system. Under capitalism production takes place on the basis of the exploitation of wage and labour. Thus lodged in the heart of the capitalist economy is a permanent conflict of interest, and this basic conflict conditions every aspect of social life. As Marx puts it in *Capital:*

> It is always the immediate relation of the owners of the conditions of production to immediate producers . . . in which we find the final secret, the hidden basis of the whole construction of society, including the political patterns of sovereignty and dependence, in short, of a given specific form of governments.[3]

In the last analysis the various other classes or social strata can act only within the framework of alternatives provided by the two major classes. In the end they must side with one class or the other. Consequently, from a marxist standpoint, the basic criterion for the assessment of political parties is not simply on which class they are based, but where they stand in the class struggle between bourgeoisie and proletariat.

But when one speaks of Marx's theory of the party, the subject is not political parties in general, but the revolutionary party which has as its aim the overthrow of capitalism—specifically one is talking about Marx's concept of a proletarian political party, because, of course, it was his view that 'the proletariat alone is a really revolutionary class . . . The other classes decay and finally disappear in the face of modem industry; the proletariat is its special and essential product.'[4] The tradesman, the artisan, the small farmer, the peasant, are all undermined by the expansion of capitalism, but the proletariat is augmented. 'In proportion as the bourgeoisie, i.e. capital, is developed, in the same proportion is the proletariat, the modern working class, developed.'[5] The scale of production increases and so workers are drawn together in larger and larger units. 'With the development of industry the proletariat not only increases in number, it becomes concentrated in greater masses, its strength grows, and it feels its strength more.' The proletariat therefore stands at the centre of the economic structure. Potentially it is the most powerful exploited class in history. This power gives the proletariat the capacity for self-emancipation, a capacity which is a vital element in Marx's theory of revolution.[6] The second and equally important factor in Marx's assessment of the proletariat is his view that the proletariat is the first class whose victory would result not in a new form of class society, but in the abolition of all classes. This view is based on the necessarily collective nature of the proletarian struggle. Odd exceptions apart, the individual worker cannot approach his employer and ask for a wage increase with any chance of success; he is forced to combine with his fellows. The worker has no property in the means of production and he cannot obtain it as an individual, for modern industry cannot be divided up and parcelled out in millions of pieces. To capture the means of production the working class must do it collectively, through social ownership.

Marx's insistence on the proletariat as the only revolutionary class and his reasons for it are well illustrated by his attitude to the other most obvious candidate for the title, the peasantry. In Marx's day the peasantry formed the vast majority even in most European countries and were at least as poor and down-trodden as the proletariat. Moreover, there was a long tradition of violent peasant revolts. But Marx discounted all this because of the individual and fragmented nature of the peasant way of life.

> The small-holding peasants form a vast mass, the members of which live in similar conditions but without entering into manifold relations with one another. Their mode of production isolates them from one another instead of bringing them into mutual intercourse . . . In this way, the great mass of the French nation is formed by simple addition of homologous magnitudes, much as potatoes in a sack form a sack of potatoes. Insofar as millions of families live under economic conditions of existence that separate their mode of life, their interests and their culture from those of other classes, and put them in hostile opposition to the latter, they form a class. Insofar as there is merely a local interconnection among these small-holding peasants, and the identity of their interests begets no community, no national bond and no political organisation, they do not form a class. They are consequently incapable of enforcing their class interest in their own name, whether through a parliament or through a convention. They cannot represent themselves, they must be represented.[7]

The capacity of the proletariat, as against the peasantry, for self-representation, and therefore self-emancipation, is crucial for its status as a revolutionary class and for its capacity to create a revolutionary party.

However, one should not confuse the potentiality of the proletariat to create its own party with empirical actuality. Marx was aware of the gap between the proletariat as a class 'in itself' and the proletariat as a class 'for itself',[8] and the long road of struggle that lies between the two.

Nor did Marx fail to see the debilitating effects of competitive bourgeois society on the organisation and unity of the working class.

> Competition separates individuals from one another, not only the bourgeois but still more the workers, in spite of the fact that it brings them together. Hence it is a long time before these individuals can unite . . . Hence every organised power standing over and against these isolated individuals, who live in relationships daily reproducing this isolation, can only be overcome after long struggles.[9]

He recognised also the power of bourgeois ideology.

> The class which has the means of material production at its disposal has control at the same time over the means of mental production, so that thereby, generally speaking, the ideas of those who lack the means of mental production are subject to it.[10]

The formation of a workers' political party was therefore necessary in order to combat these powerful tendencies towards fragmentation and to establish the independence of the proletariat as a class. Indeed Marx often suggests that the workers cannot be regarded as a class in the full sense of the word until they have created their own distinct party. Thus we find in *The Communist Manifesto* that 'the organisation of the proletarians into a class, and consequently into a political party, is continually being upset again by the competition between the workers themselves',[11] and in the decision of the London Conference (1871) of the First International that 'the proletariat can act as a class only by constituting itself a distinct political party'.[12] This basic idea remained central to the theory and practice of both Marx and Engels from the mid-1840s to the end of their lives.

2. Communists and proletarians

This now brings us to the fundamental problem of the marxist theory of the party. Marxists believe that the class struggle is the motor of history and that 'the emancipation of the working class must be conquered by the working class themselves'.[13] At the same time they wish to create a political party to represent the historical interests of the class as a whole. What then is to be the relationship between this party and the mass of the working class? Marx addressed himself to this problem in the section of *The Communist Manifesto* entitled 'Proletarians and Communists'.

In what relation do the Communists stand to the proletarians as a whole?

The Communists do not form a separate party opposed to other working-class parties.

They have no interests separate and apart from the proletariat as a whole.

They do not set up any sectarian principles of their own, by which to shape and mould the proletarian movement.

The Communists are distinguished from the other working-class parties by this only: 1. In the national struggles of the proletarians of the different countries, they point out and bring to the front the common interests of the entire proletariat, independently of all nationality. 2. In the various stages of development which the struggle of the working class against the bourgeoisie has to pass through, they always and everywhere represent the interests of the movement as a whole.

The Communists, therefore, are on the one hand, practically, the most advanced and resolute section of the working-class parties of every country, that section which pushes forward all others; on the other hand, theoretically, they have over the great mass of the proletariat the advantage of clearly understanding the line of march, the conditions, and the ultimate general results of the proletarian movement.[14]

These few dense and brilliant paragraphs contain both the germ of the solution to the problem of the party/class relationship, and a series of broad guidelines which have shaped the practice of the marxist movement down to the present day. In the first place, absolutely ruled out is the conspiratorial view of the role of the party as a small band of adventurers acting on behalf of, but apart from, the class. Also ruled out is the authoritarian view of the party handing down orders from above to be obeyed by the essentially passive masses, and the purely propagandistic view of the sect merely preaching its doctrines until the rest of the world is won over. Firmly established is the concept of leadership won on the basis of performance in the class struggle in the service of the working class, and the principle of raising, within the everyday economic and political struggles of the workers, the overall aims of the movement. Foreshadowed in these lines are the marxist strategy of the united front,[15] the policy of working within trade unions while recognising the limitations of trade unionism, and the defence of democratic rights while striving to go beyond bourgeois democracy.

But, for all its importance, Marx's formulation contains definite limitations and lacunae. It is written at a high level of generality and nowhere deals specifically with the organisational form to be adopted by communists. Indeed it contains no clear indication of what is meant by a party. It is this original imprecision which lies behind the only proposition in the passage to have been clearly invalidated by subsequent events, namely that 'Communists do not form a separate party opposed to other working-class parties'. This makes sense as a general principle only if it is taken to be almost identical in meaning to the statement that 'they have no interests separate and apart from those of the proletariat as a whole'. Nor is this vagueness in the use of the word 'party' an isolated case confined to *The Communist Manifesto*. Throughout his work Marx uses the term party in a variety of ways (Monty Johnstone has identified at least five major 'models'[16]) to refer to such widely different phenomena as the extremely broad and loose Chartist movement, his own small group of associates and followers, and the general revolutionary cause. Thus Marx could write to Freiligrath that 'the [Communist] League, like the Society of Seasons in Paris and a hundred other associates, was only an episode in the history of the party which grows everywhere spontaneously from the soil of modern society . . . Under the term "party", I understand party in the great historical sense of the word'.[17] And he could write to Kugelmann that the Paris Commune was 'the most glorious deed of our Party since the June insurrection in Paris [1848]'.[18]

Because of Marx's vagueness on this point it is not possible to construct or reconstruct any single or systematic theory of the party from quotations taken out of their context. The only possible procedure is to examine the actual development of Marx's political activity and to interpret his various comments on the question of the party in their historical context.[19] In doing this, one central fact has constantly to be borne in mind. Marx's lack of a clear definition of the political party is neither accidental nor the product of laziness of thought. Rather, it reflects the fact that for a large part of Marx's career political parties in the modern sense of the term did not yet exist, either for the bourgeoisie or for the proletariat. The modem mass party with its clearly defined membership, organisation and constitution is a recent phenomenon. It came into being primarily to meet the challenge of universal suffrage and fully developed bourgeois democracy, and it presupposed a substantial network of communications, mass media and literacy. Prior to this the modern political party was not required by the relatively primitive political system. All that was necessary were either loose and informal associations based on a network of local notables (usually landowners), or else small gatherings, in clubs and salons, of influential intellectuals. It is unreasonable to expect of Marx conceptions which go beyond the experience of his times. This is especially true as it is much harder to see ahead in the sphere of concrete forms of organisation than it is in the sphere of general economic and social development.

For the purpose of charting the evolution of Marx's concept of the party his political life can conveniently be divided into four main periods: 1. 1847–1850, the period of the Communist League; 2. 1850–1864, the long interlude in the class struggle; 3. 1864–1872, the International Working Men's Association; 4. 1873 onwards, the beginnings of mass social democracy.

3. The Communist League

In 1846 Marx and Engels had established Communist Correspondence Committees based in Brussels and on maintaining links with Britain, France, and Germany. It was through these committees that they made contact with the League of the Just, an international secret society composed mainly of German artisans. By 1847 the League's leaders had been won over, and Marx and Engels were invited to join. This they agreed to do on condition that the old conspiratorial forms of organisation be scrapped. The League of the Just then changed its name to The League of Communists and held a reorganisation congress in which Marx and Engels participated. The main points of the congress were the achievement of a 'thoroughly democratic' structure 'with elective and always removable boards' and the struggle against 'all hankering after conspiracy'.[20] Marx and Engels fought for a turn towards open propaganda of communist ideas within the working class. We see therefore by 1847 the coming together of a number of key ideas for the marxist theory of the party. Firstly the need of the proletariat, wherever possible, for an international organisation. Secondly the link between the class struggle, the self-emancipation of the proletariat, and the need for an internally democratic organisation which openly proclaims its aims.

The League called itself, alternatively, an international body and the 'Communist Party of Germany', but in reality it was too weak to be either a forerunner of the First International or a genuine national party. Rather, with only 200–300 members,[21] spread over several countries, it cannot be regarded as more than the embryo of a party, or, to borrow a term from Paris 1968, a '*groupuscule*'. Initially the strategy adopted was for Communists to work as far as possible inside already existing movements in the different countries. Thus in Britain Ernest Jones operated within the Chartists and in France the League's members joined the Social Democrats of Ledru-Rollin and Louis Blanc. The weakness of the League was immediately shown up when it was plunged in the all-European upheaval of 1848. As Engels notes, 'the few hundred League members vanished in the enormous mass that had been suddenly hurled into the movement'.[22] This is not to say that the League's members had nothing to offer. On the contrary, as individuals they played an important part in the development of the revolution. As Stephen Born put it to Marx, 'the League has ceased to exist and yet it exists everywhere'.[23]

Having no viable organisation as a base and a working class as yet small and politically immature combined with an extremely revolutionary situation, led Marx to depart somewhat from the main scheme set out in *The Communist Manifesto*. Instead of coming forward as the clear advocate of proletarian revolution and the representative of an independent working-class party, Marx was forced to act through the *Neue Rheinische Zeitung* as the extreme left-wing of radical democracy, working to push forward the bourgeois revolution to the point where the contradictions would open up beneath its feet.

Marx was aware of the problems inherent in his position and in April 1849, when German bourgeois radicalism had demonstrated its inability to carry forward the revolution, he and his associates, Wolff, Schapper and Becker, resigned from the Rhineland District Committee of the Democratic Associations. 'In our opinion,' they wrote, 'the present form of organisation of the democratic associations embrace too many heterogeneous elements to make possible any useful activity in furtherance of its aim. In our opinion a closer association of workers' organisations will be more useful because these organisations are composed of more homogeneous elements.'[24] From this point on the struggle for the independent political organisation of the working class became central to the theory and practice of marxism.

The rapid collapse of the German revolution prevented the immediate practical realisation of this perspective, but in the autumn of 1849 Marx, now in exile in London, reconstituted the Central Committee of the Communist League and began its reorganisation in Germany, this time, of necessity, as a secret centralised party. In March 1850, in

The Address of the Central Committee to the Communist League (commonly known as *The March Address*) Marx summed up the experience of this period and the organisational lessons to be drawn from it:

> At the same time the former firm organisation of the League was considerably slackened. A large part of the members who directly participated in the revolutionary movement believed the time for secret societies to have gone by and public activities alone sufficient. The individual circles and communities allowed their connections with the Central Committee to become loose and gradually dormant. Consequently, while the democratic party, the party of the petty bourgeoisie, organised itself more and more in Germany, the workers' party lost its only firm foothold, remained organised at the most in separate localities for local purposes and in the general movement thus came completely under the domination and leadership of the petty bourgeois democrats. An end must be put to this state of affairs, the independence of the workers must be restored . . .
>
> Reorganisation can only be carried out by an emissary and the Central Committee considers it extremely important that the emissary should leave precisely at this moment when a new revolution is impending, when the workers' party, therefore, must act in the most organised, most unanimous and most independent fashion possible if it is not to be exploited and taken in tow again by the bourgeoisie as in 1848.[25]

In some respects it is in *The March Address* that Marx makes his closest approach to Lenin's concept of a vanguard party (though of course there are still major differences). The key to these organisational proposals is that they are the product of the most direct involvement in revolutionary action that Marx was ever to experience, and that they are designed as a guide to action in a situation in which it is assumed that 'a new revolution is impending'. The plan to tighten the organisation of the League and strengthen its independence does not stand on its own as an isolated organisational device, but is an integral part of a perspective of dynamic revolutionary action in which the working class is to assume leadership in the democratic revolution and push it in a socialist direction.

> Alongside the new official governments they must establish simultaneously their own workers' governments, whether in the form of municipal committees and municipal councils or in the form of workers' clubs or workers' committees . . . Arms and ammunition must not be surrendered on any pretext; any attempt at disarming must be

frustrated, if necessary by force. Destruction of the influence of the bourgeois democrats on the workers, immediate independent and armed organisation of the workers and the enforcement of conditions as difficult and compromising as possible upon the inevitable momentary rule of the bourgeois democracy—these are the main points which the proletariat and hence the League must keep in view during and after the impending insurrection.[26]

Thus the similarity between Marx's concept of the party at this point and Lenin's fifty or more years later derives in large part from the parallels in their situation. It is no coincidence that it was from *The March Address* that Trotsky derived his theory of 'permanent revolution' and that it is from Marx and Engels' writings of this period that Lenin most frequently quotes when looking for textual support for Bolshevik tactics in the two Russian Revolutions.

But Marx never made a fetish of any particular organisational form or indeed of any particular party. As conditions changed so did his attitude. Consequently when, during the summer of 1850, it became clear that the perspective on which the organisational plans of the Address were based was false, and that there would be no early outbreak of the revolution, Marx rapidly abandoned his proposals. Almost inevitably this led to a split in the Central Committee of the League between those who recognised the ebb of the revolutionary wave and those who refused to face reality. The latter faction, led by Willich and Schapper, wished artificially to precipitate the revolution and became involved in all sorts of adventuristic emigre schemes, such as a plot for the armed invasion of Germany. This split effectively put an end to the Communist League as a meaningful organisation, and although an attempt was made to save it by transferring the Central Committee to Cologne, Marx soon resigned and shortly afterwards the League itself was dissolved.

4. The years of retreat

At this point Marx began a period of his life devoted, apart from the necessities of earning a living, almost entirely to his economic researches. He summed up his perspective for the coming years in the last issue of the *Neue Rheinische Revue* in November 1850.

In view of the general prosperity which now prevails and permits the productive forces of bourgeois society to develop as rapidly as is at all possible within the framework of bourgeois society, there can be no question of any real revolution . . . A new revolution will be made possible only as the result of a new crisis, but it is just as certain as is the coming of the crisis itself.[27]

Emigre circles have always been notorious for their petty squabbles, scandals and internecine strife, therefore it was essential for Marx's psychological survival and the success of his theoretical work that he withdrew from this debilitating milieu.

Marx and Engels greeted this rest from party politicking with heartfelt sighs of relief. 'I am greatly pleased', Marx wrote to Engels 'by the public, authentic isolation in which we two, you and I, now find ourselves. It corresponds completely with our position and our principles.'[28] To which Engels replied: 'At last we have again—for the first time in a long while—an opportunity to show that we do not need any support from any party of any land whatever, and that our position is totally independent of such trash.'[29] Franz Mehring warns against taking these off-hand and private remarks too seriously[30], but some commentators, notably Bertram D. Wolfe[31] and Shlomo Avineri,[32] have sought to present them as being Marx's 'real' views on the party. But this attempt involves taking these expressions of irritation out of both their overall historical context and their immediate context (i.e. that of private letters between close friends),[33] and setting them against statements that are clearly more weighed and considered and are written for public consumption. Taken literally, these and other comments by Marx and Engels could be held to imply opposition to all political activity, which is evidently ridiculous. Even during the fifties and sixties, when Marx was most deeply engrossed in *Capital*, he never completely withdrew from political life, continuing to contribute to the Chartist newspapers and keeping a watchful eye on Ernest Jones who, in 1857, he said should 'form a party, for which he must go to the factory districts'.[34]

What then were the main factors involved in Marx's 12 year absence from any political party? Firstly, there was, as already indicated, his view that bourgeois society had entered a prolonged period of stabilisation and expansion. Secondly there was the great importance he attached to his theoretical work. When approached by a German emigre in New York to revive the Communist League, Marx retorted '[I] am deeply convinced that my theoretical labours bring greater advantage to the working class than participation in organisations the time for which has passed.'[35] Thirdly, there was the great gap which separated Marx's conception of the revolutionary movement from that of the overwhelming majority of revolutionaries around at that time.

Since for Marx the driving force of history was the class struggle and his aim was the self-emancipation of the working class, the function of a party was to lead and serve the proletariat in its battles and not to 'set up any sectarian principles of their own by which to shape and mould the proletarian movement'. The revolutionary movement of the mid-nineteenth century, however, was dominated by completely alien conceptions and traditions. The dominant trends of the time were either hangovers from the conspiratorial Jacobin tradition of the French Revolution, or came from petty-bourgeois utopian socialists who believed in reconciling capital and labour on the basis of their own enlightened ideals. Both were equally elitist in their attitude to the working class, the former wishing to act behind the back of and on behalf of the class, the latter demanding that the class remain passive until all men of goodwill had been persuaded by the force of reason. Marx had long since rejected these positions and whilst he was prepared to do battle with them in the context of a living working-class movement, outside such a context, in tiny and irrelevant clubs and societies, he considered he would be wasting his time if he were to get involved with them in any way.

5. The First International—practice and theory

What finally drew Marx out of his self-imposed isolation was an invitation to the founding meeting of the International Working Men's Association held at St Martin's Hall on 26 September 1864. The International was neither founded by Marx nor marxist in inspiration. Rather it grew out of the general rise in the economic struggles of the European working class, and working-class interest in such international questions as support for the North in the American Civil War, the cause of Polish independence, and the unification of Italy, and one of its most important practical activities was preventing the use of immigrant labour to break strikes. The immediate initiative for the St Martin's Hall meeting came from trade unionists in London and Paris. But it was precisely this authenticity and spontaneity which attracted Marx. 'I knew,' he wrote to Engels, 'that this time real "powers" were involved both on the London and Paris sides and therefore decided to waive my usual standing rule to decline any such invitations . . . for a revival of the working classes is now evidently taking place.'[36]

Inevitably these positive features had their negative side in extreme theoretical and political heterogeneity and confusion. Among those participating in the International were followers of Mazzini who were essentially Italian nationalists, French Proudhonists who wanted to reconcile capital and labour, Owenites like Weston[37] who opposed strikes, and secret societies, outwardly of masonic form, such as the Philadelphians.[38] In order to work with this amorphous body and steer it along the lines he wanted, Marx was obliged to operate with great tact and not a little deviousness. Having manoeuvred himself into the job of drawing up the International's Rules, and managing to slip in his own 'Inaugural Address',[39] a considerable amount of compromise was needed to avoid alienating the other participants.

> It was very difficult to frame the thing so that our view should appear in a form acceptable from the present standpoint of the workers' movement. In a few weeks the same people will be holding meetings for the franchise with Bright and Cobden. It will take time before the reawakened movement allows the old boldness of speech. It will be necessary to be *fortiter in re, suaviter in modo*.[40]

Marx's method was to stress the class character of the movement and its internationalism, with emphasis on the then popular theme of self-emancipation,[41] without being specific as to revolutionary aims or methods. Thus the Rules state that 'the emancipation of the working classes must be conquered by the working classes themselves', and that 'the economical emancipation of the working classes is therefore the great end to which every political movement ought to be subordinate as a means', and that 'the emancipation of labour is neither a local nor a national, but a social problem, embracing all countries in which modern society exists'.[42] But they do not mention collectivisation of the means of production, which would have upset the Proudhonists, or revolution, which would have frightened the English trade unionists. This strategy worked very well. The International avoided becoming, in Mehring's phrase, 'a small body with a large head',[43] but at the same time Marx, by virtue of his superior overall view of the movement, gradually established his intellectual hegemony on the General Council. As the International grew in strength, benefiting particularly from the wave of strike struggles precipitated by the economic crisis of 1866–67, so Marx persuaded successive congresses to adopt progressively more socialist policies. The Congress of Lausanne (1867) passed the resolution: 'The social emancipation of the workmen is inseparable from their political emancipation.'[44] The Brussels Congress (1868) saw the defeat of the Proudhonists over the collective ownership of land, railways, mines and forests; and the London Conference (1871) decided to add to the Rules the statement that:

> In its struggle against the collective power of the possessing classes the proletariat can act as a class only by constituting itself a distinct political party opposed to all the old parties formed by the possessing classes.
>
> This constitution of the proletariat into a political party is indispensible to ensure the triumph of the Social Revolution and of its ultimate goal: the abolition of classes.[45]

But despite these advances the International remained an amalgam of too many divergent tendencies for it to become anything approaching an international communist party, nor did Marx ever attempt to impose such a conception on it. Rather he accepted that the International could be no more than a broad federation of workers' organisations and parties in different countries and that it should 'let every section freely shape its own theoretical programme'.[46]

This very looseness, which was the International's strength in that it enabled Marx to hold together its various factions while at the same time providing general guidance, was also its weakness in that it made the International an easy target for infiltration by Mikhail Bakunin and his anarchist International Brotherhood, which, in the guise of the International Alliance of Socialist Democracy, entered the International in 1868, and proved to be a major factor in its eventual collapse. Bakunin was a romantic adventurer and conspirator rather than a theorist, and the programme he put forward was naïve and confused. He advocated the 'equality of classes', the immediate abolition of the state, the abolition of the right of inheritance as the principal demands of the movement, and above all complete abstention from politics. Marx viewed these ideas with contempt—'a hash superficially scraped together from the Right and from the Left . . . this children's primer . . . the mess he has brewed from bits of Proudhon, Saint-Simon and others'[47]—but did not deny the anarchists the right to argue their case within the International. It was a dispute, not about doctrine, but about the kind of organisation the International was to be, which lay at the root of the damaging conflict between Marx and Bakunin. Bakunin, exploiting the numerous tensions and divisions in the International, launched a campaign against the 'authoritarianism' of the General Council which was calculated to gather the various malcontents around it. But within the framework of this 'anti-authoritarianism' Bakunin sought to realise the unelected 'collective and invisible dictatorship'[48] of his own secret societies and conspiracies. The real issue was, as Monty Johnstone says, 'whether the International should be run as a public democratic organisation in accordance with rules and policies laid down at its congresses or whether it should allow Bakunin to "paralyse its action by secret intrigue", and federations and sections to refuse to accept congress decisions with which they disagreed.'[49]

The activities of Bakunin assumed the importance they did because they intersected with the other major factor in the demise of the International, the Paris Commune. Marx's passionate vindication of the Commune in *The Civil War in France* led to the identification of the International with the Commune, and hence to a massive 'red scare' and witch-hunt against the International throughout Europe. At the same time, this appearance of the social revolution in reality, and the consequent clarity with which political questions were posed, inevitably shattered the flimsy unity on which the International was based.

To deal with this situation Marx, at the London Conference, asked for and obtained increased powers for the General Council, but this in turn threw those who resented the 'interference' of the General Council into the camp of Bakunin's anti-authoritarianism. By 1872 Marx, it is clear, had decided that the International had had its day (though he did not care to say so publicly). At the same time he was determined that it should not fall into the hands of conspirators, either Bakuninist or Blanquist, who would compromise the positive achievements of the International with pointless adventures. Marx achieved these aims at the Hague Congress by securing the expulsion of Bakunin (on a rather dubious basis),[50] and by having the seat of the International transferred to America where it passed away peacefully in 1876.

The International Working Men's Association was undoubtedly the most important practical political work of Marx's life. It gave a great impetus to the development of the movement everywhere. It created a much more widespread awareness of at least some of Marx's basic principles than had ever existed before. Above all, it established the tradition of internationalism and of international organisation at the heart of the working-class socialist movement. These were great achievements, but it is also evident that the International contained the seeds of its disintegration in the basis of its foundation. From the point of view of assessing Marx's concept of the party, it is necessary therefore to examine the strengths and weaknesses of the theoretical ideas which underlay his work during this period.

Since for Marx the party was always considered in relationship to the working class, and the working class is defined basically by its economic situation, the key theoretical problem was the nature of the relationship between economics and politics, and specifically between the economic struggles of the working class and the development of its political consciousness and organisation. There are various texts of the period which show that, essentially, Marx held the view that political consciousness arises spontaneously from the economic circumstances and struggle of the workers. Thus in a speech to a delegation of German trade unionists in 1869 Marx said:

> Trade unions are the schools of socialism. It is in trade unions that workers educate themselves and become socialists because under their very eyes and every day the struggle with capital is taking place . . . The great mass of workers, whatever party they belong to, have at last understood that their material situation must become better. But once the worker's material situation has become better, he can consecrate himself to the education of his children; his wife and children do not need to go to the factory; he himself can cultivate his mind more, look after his body better, and he becomes socialist without noticing it.[51]

While some of the more extreme statements here need not be taken too literally, Marx repeated essentially the same theoretical conception in a key passage in a letter to F. Bolte in 1871:

> The political movement of the working class has as its ultimate object, of course, the conquest of political power for this class, and this naturally requires a previous organisation of the working class developed up to a certain point and arising from its economic struggles.
>
> On the other hand, however, every movement in which the working class comes out as a *class* against the ruling classes and tries to coerce

them by pressure from without is a political movement. For instance, the attempt in a particular factory, or even a particular trade, to force a shorter working day out of individual capitalists by strikes, etc, is a purely economic movement. On the other hand, the movement to force through an eight-hour, etc, *law*, is a *political* movement. And, in this way, out of the separate economic movements of the workers there grows up every-where a *political* movement, that is to say, a movement of the *class*, with the effect of enforcing its interests in a general form, in a form possessing general socially coercive force [emphasis in the original].[52]

The strength of Marx's conception lies in its materialism, its emphasis on learning through experience and struggle; its weakness lies in its economic determinism and optimistic evolutionism. History has demonstrated not only the process of development outlined by Marx, but also a wide range of counteracting forces serving to block the transition from trade-union consciousness to socialist consciousness. In particular the ability of economic gains, even including those won through struggle, to serve as palliatives, not stimulants, and the grip of bourgeois ideology on the proletariat, with its consequent ability to divide and fragment the movement, were both seriously underestimated by Marx. In 1890 Engels commented that 'Marx and I are partly to blame for the fact that the younger people sometimes lay more stress on the economic side than is due to it. We had to emphasise the main principle vis-à-vis our adversaries, who denied it, and we had not always the time, the place, or the opportunity to give their due to the other elements involved in the interaction',[53] and the question of the development of socialist consciousness is one on which Marx was most guilty of overemphasising 'the main principle' at the expense of 'other elements involved in the interaction'.

It was on this oversimplified and over-optimistic view of the trans-formation of the working class from a 'class-in-itself' into a 'class-for-itself' that Marx based his ideas on organisation and his activity in the International. For Marx the main problem was to establish a political organisation based on the idea of class struggle and involving wide layers of workers. This achieved, he believed the organisation would evolve in a revolutionary direction of its own accord.

There is, therefore, a strong element of fatalism in Marx's attitude to the formation of the party. The struggle of ideas and tendencies within the working-class movement will sort itself out as the class tendencies of the workers assert themselves. The basic problem was that Marx failed to grasp the possibility of working-class political reformism (i.e. what we now call social democracy or labourism) taking a serious hold on the movement in such a way that it would not simply transform itself or make way for revolutionary action when its time was passed, but would constitute a major obstacle blocking the road to revolution. Because he did not see the danger, Marx also did not see the means of combating it—the creation of a relatively narrow and disciplined vanguard party.

6. Social democracy and the problem of reformism

From 1872 onwards Marx and Engels were never again directly involved in, or members of, any organisation or party, but they nonetheless regarded themselves as having 'special status as representatives of *international* socialism',[54] and in that capacity dispensed advice to socialists throughout the world. It was largely Engels who was active in this role, rather than Marx, whose health declined and who concentrated on his studies. But it seems reasonable, in this sphere at least, to regard Engels' views as broadly representative of Marx's.

The most important phenomenon of this period was the rise of social-democratic workers' parties in a number of countries, especially in Germany. These organisations combined an openly socialist programme with a mass following in the working class. Observation of this development, combined with the experience of the International, seems to have led to a certain reappraisal, or at least a change of emphasis, in Marx and Engels' views. Thus in 1873 we find Engels warning Bebel not 'to be misled by the cry for "unity" . . . a party proves itself victorious by *splitting* and being able to stand the split',[55] and in 1874 predicting to Sorge that 'the next International—after Marx's writings have produced their effects for some years—will be directly Communist and will proclaim precisely our principles'.[56]

In Britain and the USA, where there were very strong working classes but the workers were politically subordinate to the ruling-class parties and the socialist currents were extremely weak, Marx and Engels continued with their old line of advocating the formation of a broad independent workers' party without worrying about its programme or theoretical basis. Engels wrote a series of articles to this effect in *The Labour Standard* in 1881, arguing, in an anticipation of the way the Labour Party was to arise, that 'at the side of, or above, the Unions of

special trades there must spring up a general union, a political organisation of the working class as a whole',[57] and in 1893 he urged all
socialists to join the Independent Labour Party. In relation to America,
Engels argued that:

> The great thing is to get the working class to move *as a class;* that once
> obtained they will soon find the right direction . . . To expect the
> Americans to start with the full consciousness of the theory worked out
> in older industrial countries is to expect the impossible . . . A million or
> two working men's votes next November for a bona fide working men's
> party is worth infinitely more at present than a hundred thousand votes
> for a doctrinally perfect platform . . . But anything that might delay or
> prevent that national consolidation of the workingmen's party—on no
> matter what platform—I should consider a great mistake.[58]

But where France and Germany were concerned, where the movement was much more advanced, Marx and Engels' attitude was very different. Here they saw the possibility, for the first time, of the creation
of substantial marxist parties in the shape of the Parti Ouvrier Français
and the German SDAP, and so as to realise that possibility they paid
particular attention to questions of theory and programme. Thus when
in 1882 the French party split between the marxists led by Guesde and
Lafargue and 'possibilists' led by Malon and Brousse (anarchists turned
reformists), Engels welcomed the event as 'inevitable' and 'a good thing',
maintaining that 'the sham St Etienne party [the possibilists] is not only
no workers' party but no party whatever because in actual fact it has no
programme',[59] and commenting 'it seems that *every* workers' party of a
big country can develop only through internal struggle, which accords
with the laws of dialectical development in general'.[60] But above all it
was in their dealings with German social democracy that Marx and
Engels maintained the highest degree of theoretical rigour.

When in 1875 the SDAP united with the Lassallean ADAV to
form the German Social-Democratic Workers' Party (SAPD, later
SPD), Marx and Engels opposed this move as 'precipitate on our part'[61]
and involving theoretical concessions. Marx immediately subjected
the unification programme to a devastating critique,[62] exposing not
only the reactionary implications of Lassallean formulations such as
the 'iron law of wages', 'equal rights to the undiminished proceeds of
labour' and 'producers' cooperatives with state aid', but also taking up

the whole question of the class nature of the state in opposition to the call for a 'free people's state', condemning the programme for its lack of internationalism, and complaining that 'there is nothing in its political demands beyond the old and generally familiar democratic litany: universal suffrage, direct legislation, popular justice, a people's army, etc.'[63] In 1877 Engels, to preserve the hegemony of marxism in the German movement, undertook the huge *Anti-Dühring* project, and in 1879 Marx and Engels dispatched a 'Circular Letter' to party leaders protesting in the strongest possible terms at the emergence within the party of non-proletarian tendencies which rejected the class struggle and hence the class nature of the party, and 'openly state that the workers are too uneducated to emancipate themselves and must be freed from above by philanthropic big bourgeois and petty bourgeois'.[64] Also in 1879 they objected to 'Liebknecht's untimely weakness in the Reichstag'[65] in the face of Bismarck's anti-socialist law, and to the opportunistic support of Bismarck's protectionist tariff policy by the SAPD parliamentary group, in response to which Marx declared 'they are already so much affected by parliamentary idiotism that they think they are *above criticism*.'[66]

But this continuous stream of criticism should not deceive. It reflected not hostility to German social democracy but Marx and Engels' exceptional interest in and concern for the organisation which they repeatedly refer to as 'our party'. Despite their vehement attacks on every *open* manifestation of reformism and capitulation to bourgeois democracy, Marx and Engels remained attached to the German party by 'bonds of solidarity'[67] and so, with their blessing, it became for the rest of the world *the* model of a marxist party. What Marx and Engels failed to grasp was that the main danger lay not in what the party said, but in what it did, in what it essentially was. This problem was highlighted a few years later in the so-called 'revisionist debate' when Bernstein demanded that the party adopt an openly reformist stance. In a very perceptive letter the Bavarian socialist, Ignaz Auer, wrote to Bernstein: 'My dear Ede, one doesn't formally decide to do what you ask, one doesn't say it, one *does* it. Our whole activity—even under the shameful anti-socialist law—was the activity of a social-democratic reforming party. A party which reckons with the masses simply cannot be anything else.'[68] The root of the problem lay in the conception of the relationship between the party and the working class, a conception which neither Marx nor Engels ever clearly challenged; i.e. that of a broad party steadily and smoothly expanding, organising within ever wider sections of the proletariat, until at last it embraced the overwhelming majority.

As Chris Harman has written: 'What is central for the social democrat is that the party *represents* the class.'[69] If the party represents the class, then it must contain within it the different tendencies existing within the class, and Marx and Engels, though they strove for the dominance of marxism, accepted this. Thus Engels wrote in 1890: 'The party is so big that absolute freedom of debate inside it is a necessity . . . The greatest party in the land cannot exist without all shades of opinion in it making themselves fully felt.'[70] If the party represents the class during a period of capitalist expansion and stability in which the mass of the working class is reformist, then the party must be reformist too, even if it does not openly admit it. But reformist workers and reformist political leaders are not at all the same thing. The consciousness of the average worker is a mixture of many often contradictory elements and so under the stimulus of his material needs, his direct involvement in the struggle, and dramatic changes in the political situation, it is possible for his consciousness to change very rapidly. The consciousness of the leader, however, is much more definitely formed and coherent (it is this which makes him a leader) and therefore much more resistant to change; moreover the leader is not subject to the same material pressures as the worker, but rather is likely to have carved out for himself a position of privilege (e.g. as MP or trade-union leader). The consequence is that the relationship of representing the working class in its reformist phase turns into opposing and betraying it in its revolutionary phase. To be with the class in a revolutionary situation the party has to be somewhat ahead of it in the pre-revolutionary period. The party does not cease to represent the *interests* of the class as a whole, but to do this it has to restrict its membership to those for whom the interests of the class as a whole predominate over individual, sectional, national or immediate advantage, i.e. to revolutionaries.

That Marx never fully developed or articulated this idea, really the essential starting point for a theory of the *revolutionary* party, is rooted in what we called earlier the 'optimistic evolutionism' of his view of the growth of working-class political consciousness, which he saw as rising relatively smoothly and evenly, roughly in proportion to the develop- ment of capitalism. That Marx did not progress beyond this view is not, however, surprising, or something for which he can be blamed. For the greater part of Marx's life the problem of reformism had not emerged as in any way a major threat; the main tasks were overcoming the petty bourgeois, sectarian, conspiratorial and utopian socialist traditions of revolutionary organisation inherited from the French Revolution, and establishing the political independence of the proletariat. Marx's contribution to the achievement of these tasks by the proletariat in most European countries was immense. If in the course of the struggle he 'bent-the-stick' in the direction of economic determinism, then this is perfectly understandable. But it is also necessary to understand that in the sphere of his theory of the party, the legacy of Marx's work, whatever its positive achievements, was something that had in time to be overcome by the marxist movement if capitalism was to be overthrown.

2.
Lenin and the birth of Bolshevism

Although marxism in general is, as Gramsci put it, a 'philosophy of action' and thus hostile to fatalism, Marx himself, as we have shown, owing to the prevailing conditions and his determination to avoid sectarianism never fully emancipated himself from a fatalist conception of political organisation. The political party of the proletariat would emerge gradually, spontaneously, from the broad struggle of the working class. In social democracy this fatalist tendency thoroughly consolidated itself in the sphere of organisation and then extended itself to the theory of capitalist development, the proletarian revolution, and the nature of human activity itself. The practice of Bolshevism and the organisational ideas of Lenin marked a break with this fatalism, and thus constituted a tremendous step forward for marxist theory not only in relation to social democracy but also in relation to Marx. Only with Lenin was the concept of a broad party that *represents*, or *is*, the working class replaced by that of a 'minority' party (in the pre-revolutionary period) which is the *vanguard* of the class and which, since it is the organisational embodiment of the socialist future of that class, has a duty to defend itself from and struggle against all manifestations of opportunism.

1. The background to Bolshevism

Bolshevism was no 'Venus' born fully grown from the waves—it developed and grew through a host of struggles, internal and external. Nor can it be seen simply as the product of Lenin's organisational genius. The idealisation of Lenin that is general in marxist circles combined with the tendency of Stalinist theoreticians to write Russian revolutionary history as though there were only two protagonists, the Russian people and Lenin

31

(most other individuals having become unpersons), has created an image of Bolshevism as invented by Lenin much as Watt invented the steam engine. In fact the break with gradualism in the sphere of organisation was itself a gradual and only semi-conscious process, though one marked by many sharp and conscious struggles. Leninism was the product of a sustained and developing revolutionary response to a concrete situation, and to understand that response we must look at the elements in the situation that made it possible.

The first factor which springs to mind as a source of Bolshevism is what Tony Cliff calls 'the tradition of substitutionism in the Russian revolutionary movement'.[1] This tradition was indeed very strong. In the 1860s and 1870s sometimes tens, occasionally hundreds, of heroic and idealistic intellectuals pitted themselves against the autocracy, alternatively 'going to the people' as their educators and enlighteners and 'acting on behalf of the people' with daring acts of terrorism. And in so doing these Narodniks gained the undying respect and admiration of Russian revolutionaries including Lenin especially, who refers repeatedly to their 'devoted determination and vigour'.[2] To strengthen the case various pieces of biographical evidence can be thrown in: the formative influence on Lenin of such basically elitist writers as Chernychevsky and Tkachev,[3] and of course the fate of his brother, executed for terrorism.

However, this argument, superficially attractive as it is, will not bear critical examination. It ignores the fact that Lenin cut his theoretical teeth precisely in the struggle against Narodism; that he opposed individual terrorism throughout his life; that he refused to countenance a seizure of power in 1917 until the Bolsheviks had a majority in the soviets; and that he waged a most vigorous struggle against all forms of 'putchism', of attempts at uprisings by minorities, at the third Congress of the Communist International (1921).

It was not terrorism but the situation which produced terrorism that was an important factor in the development of Lenin's ideas. Lenin could break decisively with the romantic and utopian theories of the terrorists, he could adhere absolutely to the theory of the class struggle as the lever of the social revolution, but he could not break with the reality of the Tsarist police. Under Tsarism political repression remained virtually absolute and so did the ban on all trade-union and strike activity.

In such a situation the social-democratic model of a broad mass party representing the whole of the working class was simply impossible. 'Only an incorrigible utopian would have a *broad* organisation of workers . . . under the autocracy'.[4] In fact as far as combating the Tsarist police was concerned, the *smaller* the organisation the better. Inextricably linked to the question of size and secrecy was the need for efficiency and vigorous training. Need for efficiency which is hammered home again and again in *What is to be done?*, and which was almost certainly the main objective factor in determining the success of this work at the time, gives rise to the concept of the professional revolutionary as the basis of the revolutionary organisation. Summing up his views on this aspect of the argument Lenin writes:

> in an autocratic state, the more we *confine* the membership of such an organisation to people who are professionally engaged in revolution-ary activity and who have been professionally trained in the art of com-bating the political police, the more difficult will it be to unearth the organisation.[5]

The eminent practicality of this emphasis on secrecy, training and professionalism in organisation should be clear. But this element of pure practicality or necessity in Lenin's theory of organisation can easily be exaggerated. If immediate expediency were the sole consideration, then it would be true to say with Leonard Schapiro (and many other commentators) that 'Lenin's conceptions had perhaps moved nearer to the conspiratorial ideas of Narodnaya Volya, and away from Marx's conception of the historic mission of an entire class'.[6] In fact this was not so; the hard core of professional revolutionaries were not seen as an end in themselves but as a means. Lenin stresses that the tighter the core of the party 'the *greater* will be the number of people from the working class and from the other social classes who will be able to join the movement and perform active work in it'.[7] Lenin's perspective was *always* one of a mass class movement against the autocracy but one led by a vanguard party. 'We are the party of a class, and therefore *almost the entire class* (and in times of war, in a period of civil war, the entire class) should act under the leadership of our party.'[8] Furthermore, if it were merely practical necessity that determined Lenin's thought, then his ideas would possess only local, temporary significance. Bolshevism would have proved a specifically Russian phenomenon, an exception to the rule, rather than the basis for a vast international movement and tradition. Indeed the conspiratorial elements in Lenin's conception *are* historically limited and Lenin recognises this.

> Under conditions of political freedom our party will be built entirely on the elective principle. Under the autocracy this is impracticable for the collective thousands of workers that make up the party.[9]

If it was the level of repression that made a broad Western-type party impossible, it was the particular social and political conjuncture in Russia and trends within the revolutionary movement that stimulated Lenin into new theoretical insights and enabled him to take a step forward from the social-democratic model rather than a step backwards to conspiracy. This situation must therefore be examined.

The primary distinction between the tasks of the revolutionary movement in Western Europe and in Russia was that in the West capitalism had been firmly established, whereas in Russia capitalism was still nascent and the bourgeois revolution had not yet been achieved. Thus whereas in the West marxism presented itself straightforwardly as the theory of the overthrow of capitalism by the proletariat, in Russia marxism appeared to many as the theory of the inevitability of the development of capitalism. Since the authorities at first regarded the terrorists as the main danger and the terrorists argued that Russia could side-step capitalism by means of an immediate revolution, marxist criticism of terrorism and emphasis on the inevitability of capitalism was for a period welcomed or at least regarded as very much a lesser evil. This led to what became known as 'legal marxism', and marxism became a veritable fashion:

> Marxist journals and newspapers were founded, nearly everyone became a marxist, marxists were flattered, marxists were courted, and the book publishers rejoiced at the extraordinary ready sale of marxist literature.[10]

Inevitably in such a situation a coalition of 'manifestly heterogeneous elements'[11] occurred. In particular calling themselves marxists were those who regarded capitalism as inevitable and progressive but who also wanted to fight it and overthrow it, and also calling themselves marxists were those who in reality supported capitalism as such and for whom socialism was cloudy rhetoric for the dim and distant future. (The leading representative of the latter trend was Pyotr Struve, originally a collaborator of Lenin and Plekhanov, who was, in 1905, to found the bourgeois-democratic Cadet Party.) This meant that from very early on Lenin felt himself in the position of having to select very rigorously those who really wanted to fight from a large number of people who mouthed radical phrases. This was a major factor in conditioning Lenin's doctrinal intransigence and especially his insistence on distinguishing between what people said and what they were actually prepared to do. This latter faculty, which was so acutely developed in Lenin and is one of the most striking features of all his writings, was to play an enormous role in the development of Bolshevism as a separate party.

The revolutionary marxist answer to the problem of seeing capitalism as progressive and at the same time maintaining the complete independence of the proletariat for the fight against capitalism lay in the theory of the hegemony of the proletariat in the bourgeois revolution. Originating in Plekhanov ('the Russian revolution will succeed as a workers' revolution or it will not succeed at all')[12], though later abandoned by him, and adopted and refined by Lenin, this theory was to become a hallmark of Bolshevism in the pre-1917 period. The essence of this theory was that the Russian bourgeoisie arrived late on the scene, long after the bourgeoisie had ceased to be a revolutionary force on a world scale. Consequently the task of leading a revolution against the autocracy would fall to a proletariat which, although small, was developing rapidly in large scale modern industry and could ally itself to the tremendous elemental force of the peasant revolt.[13] In order to accomplish this task the proletariat would have to adopt the overthrow of Tsarism as its first and most important demand and place itself in the vanguard of every struggle for democracy and political freedom.

2. The critique of 'economism'

It was this theory which brought Lenin into conflict with the various trends which he grouped under the term 'economism'. The main representatives of 'economism' at the time were *Rabochaya Mysl* (*The Workers' Thought*), a journal published in St Petersburg from 1897 to 1902, and *Rabocheye Dyelo* (*The Workers' Task*), the organ of the Union of Russian Social Democrats Abroad from 1899 to 1903—the latter assuming a position which could more strictly be described as semi-'economist'. The basic contention of the 'economists' was that social democracy should concentrate its work not on the political struggle against the autocracy, but in serving and developing the economic struggle of the workers, and it was from the disputes with 'economism' that many of the fundamental ideas of Bolshevism emerged. In order to understand and assess those ideas it will therefore be necessary to look at the disputes in some detail—but even before that it is necessary to look at the *context* in which the disputes occurred and simply to ask *why* they were so important.

The basic reason was that Lenin saw 'economism' as leading inevitably to the abandonment of the hegemony of the proletariat in the coming democratic revolution by instituting a division of labour in which the workers would limit themselves to the trade-union struggle, leaving politics to the bourgeoisie. Indeed it was the open advocacy of such a division in the document known as 'The Credo', by Y. D. Kuskova of the Union of Russian Social Democrats Abroad, that first spurred Lenin to take up the cudgels against 'economism' with his 'Protest by Russian Social Democrats' in August 1899.[14] In 'The Credo' Kuskova had written: 'For the Russian marxist there is only one course: participation in, i.e. assistance to, the economic struggle of the proletariat; and participation in liberal opposition activity.'[15]

To Lenin such a course meant betrayal of the revolution, for 'liberal opposition activity' (i.e. the bourgeoisie) was completely incapable of consistent revolutionary opposition to the autocracy. He held that any attempt to narrow down the tasks of the proletariat and the social-democratic movement would play into the hands of the bourgeoisie, and regarded *any* tendency towards 'economism' as leading in that direction. In this way the debate over 'economism' foreshadowed the central issue for the Russian marxists during the next 17 years—the relative role and tasks of the bourgeoisie and the proletariat in the revolution—with a fundamental continuity existing between the position of early 'economism' and late Menshevism that the leading role should go to the bourgeoisie.

From this it can be seen that Lenin was also correct in linking 'economism' to the international trend to reformism or 'revisionism' in social democracy, which he does right at the beginning of *What is to be done?* The 'economists' shared the de facto split between economics and politics and asserted with Bernstein the importance of 'the movement' (immediate demands) as against the 'ultimate aim' (socialism or, in this case, the overthrow of Tsarism).

Fierce polemic, for Lenin, meant getting to the very root of the disputed questions and pursuing ruthlessly the logic of his own and his opponents' arguments; thus these polemics, though rooted in concrete issues, invariably possess a certain universal significance.[16] The product of the struggle against the 'economists' was *What is to be done?* which, quite deservedly, has had an immense influence on marxist theory and practice throughout the world and which, I would argue, has wrongly been regarded as *the* standard marxist text on the theory of the party. Thus any critical study of the marxist theory of the party must look very seriously at this work.

What is to be done? sums up all Lenin's arguments against 'economism' and his case for a nationwide revolutionary organisation based on a cadre of professional revolutionaries and an all-Russia newspaper. Thus many of the points it makes are of a practical nature of the kind referred to earlier in this essay, but its central theme is the relationship of spontaneity and consciousness in the development of the revolutionary movement. The 'economists', holding that 'politics always obediently follows economics'[17] and that therefore political consciousness would grow organically from economic struggles, contended that the main task of marxists was to assist the economic struggle, and that Lenin and the Iskraists 'belittled the spontaneous element' and 'overestimated consciousness'. But for Lenin even this method of presenting the problem was completely unsatisfactory. It was not that the spontaneous upsurge of the workers was unimportant (on the contrary it was profoundly important), but that its importance lay precisely in the demands that it made on consciousness, on organisation.

The programme of *Rabocheye Dyelo* stated:

We consider that the most important phenomenon of Russian life, the one that will mainly determine the tasks and the character of the publication activity of the Union, is the mass working-class movement which has arisen in recent years.

And Lenin comments:

That the mass movement is a most important phenomenon is not to be disputed. But the crux of the matter is, how is one to understand the statement that the mass working-class movement will 'determine the tasks'? It may be interpreted in one of two ways. *Either* it means bowing to the spontaneity of this movement, i.e. reducing the role of social democracy to mere subservience to the working-class movement as such—*or* it means that the mass movement places before us *new* theoretical, political, and organisational tasks, far more complicated than those that might have satisfied us in the period before the rise of the mass movement.[18]

This dialectical conception of the relationship between spontaneity and consciousness, the mass movement and the party, represents a tremendous step forward for marxist theory and is an advance on any previous contribution to this problem (including that of Marx himself and especially that of German Social Democracy). Essentially it is the necessary starting point of a truly revolutionary theory of the party because it is a radical break with *fatalism*.[19] 'We revolutionary social democrats, on the contrary, are dissatisfied with this worship of spontaneity, i.e. *of that which exists "at the present moment"*' [My emphasis—J.M.][20]

For Lenin the development of the class struggle itself, even its economic form, is a process of moving from 'spontaneity' to 'consciousness'.

Strikes occurred in Russia in the seventies and sixties (and even in the first half of the nineteenth century) and they were accompanied by the 'spontaneous' destruction of machinery, etc. Compared with these 'revolts', the strikes of the nineties might even be described as 'conscious', to such an extent do they mark the progress which the working-class movement made in that period. This shows that the 'spontaneous element' in essence, represents nothing more nor less than consciousness in *embryonic* form.[21]

Lenin therefore sees it as the duty of the revolutionary always to assist the conscious element and work to overcome spontaneity.

But Lenin is not merely arguing for organisation against lack of organisation, for leadership against the 'tail-ending' (tailism) of the 'economists'. What is central to his attack on the 'economists' and to his view of the nature of tasks of the party is his rejection of the notion that proletarian class-consciousness can develop gradually on the basis of an accumulation of economic struggles.

As Lukacs writes:

The impossibility of the economic evolution of capitalism into socialism was clearly proved by the Bernstein debates. Nevertheless, its ideological counterpart lived on uncontradicted in the minds of many honest European revolutionaries, and was, moreover, not even recognised as either a problem or a danger.[22]

Lenin's position on this was extreme and uncompromising.

Working-class consciousness cannot be genuine political consciousness unless the workers are trained to respond to *all* cases of tyranny, oppression, violence, and abuse, no matter *what* class is affected—unless they are trained, moreover, to respond from a social-democratic point of view and no other. The consciousness of the working masses cannot be genuine class-consciousness, unless the workers learn, from concrete, and above all from topical, political facts and events to observe *every* other social class in all the manifestations of its intellectual, ethical and political life; unless they learn to apply in practice the materialist analysis and the materialist estimate of *all* aspects of the life and activity of *all* classes, strata and groups of the population.[23]

And therefore:

Class political consciousness can be brought to the workers *only from without*, that is, only from outside the economic struggle, from outside the sphere of relations between workers and employers.[24]

In practical terms this meant that it was necessary for social democrats not merely 'to go among the workers', but to 'go among all classes of the population; they must dispatch units of their army *in all directions*'.[25] Workers should be mobilised to take action in support of all victims of the autocracy including such groups as religious minorities and students. 'The social democrats' ideal should not be the trade-union secretary, but *the tribune of the people* . . . who is able to take advantage of every event, however small, in order to set forth *before all* his socialist convictions and his democratic demands.'[26] Essential to this strategy was an all-Russia newspaper keeping a vigilant eye on every aspect of political and social life in Russia and able to mount nationwide political exposures. 'Without a political organ, a political movement deserving that name is inconceivable in the Europe of today.'[27]

It is perhaps necessary to point out in passing that of course Lenin in no way regarded this diversification of forces as a modification or compromise of the class basis of the party. On the contrary, it was possible only on the basis of a prolonged period of largely economistic agitation in the working class. 'In the earlier period, indeed, we had astonishingly few forces, and it was perfectly natural and legitimate then to devote ourselves exclusively to activities among the workers and to condemn severely any deviation from this course. The entire task then was to consolidate our position in the working class.'[28] And in any case the whole purpose of the strategy was to ensure the hegemony of the proletariat in the struggle against the autocracy.

What is specifically and characteristically Leninist about this approach, and what distinguishes it from the methods of social democracy and the Second International, is *not* that marxists fight for democratic rights and for reforms. That much was common ground and indeed second nature to German Social Democracy. But the social democrats fought for reforms because they were 'progressive' and part of the development of capitalism into socialism; in other words, they fought for reforms *as reformists*. Whereas, for Lenin, the whole process was part of the battle for the class-consciousness of the proletariat, to enable it to grasp the relationships in action of all social classes and groups, and thus to fit itself for taking power. Thus for social democracy a yawning gap developed between the minimum and the maximum programme (between immediate demands and ultimate aim). While, for Lenin, all-sided political agitation was a means of bridging this gap and securing the predominance of the ultimate *revolutionary* aim.

3. Socialism from without?

At this point, we have summed up the main advances made by *What is to be done?* over the theory of the party to be found in Marx and prevailing in more dogmatic form in Russian 'economism' and to a certain extent in European social democracy. But there remains an important aspect of Lenin's argument we have not dealt with—important not because of its centrality to Lenin's own theory and practice, but because of its influence on many later followers. We are referring to the thesis that 'political consciousness' can only be introduced into the working-class movement 'from without', which is inserted to give theoretical justification to the attack on spontaneism. This thesis appears in *What is to be done?* in two forms. One, which we have cited already, is that:

> Class political consciousness can be brought to the workers *only from without*, that is, only from outside the economic struggle, from outside the sphere of relations between workers and employers.

The other is that:

We have said that *there could not have been* social-democratic consciousness among the workers. It would have to be brought to them from without. The history of all countries shows that the working class, exclusively by its own effort, is able to develop only trade-union consciousness i.e. the conviction that it is necessary to combine in unions, fight the employers, and strive to compel the government to pass necessary labour legislation, etc. The theory of socialism, however, grew out of the philosophic, historical, and economic theories elaborated by educated representatives of the propertied classes, by intellectuals. By their social status, the founders of modem scientific socialism, Marx and Engels, themselves belonged to the bourgeois intelligentsia. In the very same way, in Russia, the theoretical doctrine of social democracy arose altogether independently of the spontaneous growth of the working-class movement; it arose as a natural and inevitable outcome of the development of thought among the revolutionary socialist intelligentsia.[29]

There is a clear distinction between the two formulations. The first is merely an extreme and slightly clumsy way of saying that workers need to understand the totality of social relations and all forms of oppression, knowledge of which comes from a much wider sphere than ('from without') the factory. As such, one could quibble with the wording but the content is fairly unexceptionable. In the second formulation, however, 'from without' means from outside the working class, specifically from the bourgeois intelligentsia, and moreover it carries with it an attempt at a positive account of the origins and development of the theory of scientific socialism. This raises problems of considerable theoretical significance, especially for the theory of the party, so it is necessary to embark on a fairly detailed critical analysis of Lenin's conception here.

The first point that must be made is that Lenin was here expressing ideas taken directly from Karl Kautsky, and indeed he uses a quotation from Kautsky to provide himself with theoretical authority.

> But socialism and the class struggle arise side by side and not one out of the other; each arises under different conditions. Modern socialist consciousness can arise only on the basis of profound scientific knowledge. Indeed modern economic science is as much a condition for socialist production as, say, modern technology, and the proletariat can create neither the one nor the other, no matter how much it may desire to do so; both arise out of the modern social process. The vehicle of science is not the proletariat but the bourgeois intelligentsia.[30]

This resort to Kautsky, given the latter's mechanical version of marxism and his subsequent political development, is clearly a danger signal to those of us working with the benefit of hindsight, and a number of latter-day Leninists have been critical of this point. Trotsky comments that Lenin himself 'subsequently acknowledged the biased nature, and therewith the erroneousness, of his theory'.[31] Lucio Magri in a recent article calls the quotation from Kautsky an 'enlightenment schema',[32] and Nigel Harris refers to it as an 'elitist statement'.[33]

The fundamental problem is that if one accepts literally the Lenin-Kautsky formulation that political consciousness derives from the bourgeois intelligentsia and at the same time that the political struggle must predominate over the economic struggle, then precious little is left of Marx's fundamental dictum that 'the emancipation of the working class is the act of the working class itself'; on the contrary the role of the working class would be a strictly subordinate one. The truly revolutionary class would be not the working class but the discontented intellectuals, thus implicitly confirming the typical bourgeois picture of radical movements as made up of a malevolent middle-class leadership and an 'innocent' manipulated working-class rank-and-file. The division of mental and manual labour inherent in class society, far from being overcome, is carried over into the socialist movement and sanctified in the revolutionary party.

In fact the whole presentation of science, theory and socialist consciousness (which are here equated) is completely un-marxist and has more in common with nineteenth century positivism and idealism. Science is seen as developing in complete isolation from social life, from practice. As far as the natural sciences, philosophy and bourgeois social science are concerned, this appears to be true insofar as the thinker tends to the isolation of the ivory tower, but in reality this is only an illusion, a mystification produced by class society. For this reason Marx refused to recognise philosophy or any other discipline as having its own history independent of the history of men active in society. Where the theory of socialism is concerned, even the relative and illusory autonomy of bourgeois science does not and should not exist if this theory is to be genuinely revolutionary. On the contrary, it must be intimately related to, influenced by and based upon the activity of the working class. Thus Marx writes:

Just as the economists are the scientific representatives of the bourgeoisie, so the socialists and communists are the theorists of the proletariat. As long as the proletariat is not sufficiently developed to constitute itself as a class, as long therefore as the struggle of the proletariat with the bourgeoisie has not acquired a political character, and while the productive forces are not yet sufficiently developed, within bourgeois society itself, to give an indication of the material conditions necessary for the emancipation of the proletariat and the constitution of a new society, these theorists remain Utopians who, in order to remedy the distress of the oppressed classes, improvise systems and pursue a regenerative science. But as history continues, and as the struggle of the proletariat takes shape more clearly, they have no further need to look for a science in their own minds; they have only to observe what is happening before their eyes, and to make themselves its vehicle of expression.[34]

Examination of the history of socialist and marxist thought also clearly refutes the 'Lenin-Kautsky' theory of 'separate development'. The idea of socialism and the socialist revolution itself was not something invented or discovered by Marx; rather it emerged from the struggles of the masses as the extreme left wing of the bourgeois revolutions in England and France—witness the Levellers and Babeuf's Conspiracy of Equals (which Marx referred to as the world's first communist party). Raya Dunayevskaya in *Marxism and Freedom* records the impact of the American Civil War and the English workers' struggle over the working day on the structure of *Capital*. She writes:

No one is more blind to the greatness of Marx's contributions than those who praise him to the skies for his genius as if that genius matured outside of the actual struggles of the period in which he lived. As if he gained the impulses from the sheer development of his own thoughts instead of from the living workers changing living reality by their actions.[35]

Indeed it was from the insurgent workers of Paris that Marx learned that the working class cannot simply take over the existing state machine but must smash it.

History also provides numerous examples of workers spontaneously rising to much greater heights than trade unionism and trade-union politics: the Chartists, the 1848 revolution in France, the Paris Commune, the Russian workers in 1905 and February 1917, the 1956 Hungarian Revolution and so on.

But this critique of the way in which Lenin theoretically justified his position at this time does not, as some of Lenin's hagiographers might maintain, undermine the whole basis of Lenin's theory of the party. The fact of workers achieving socialist consciousness spontaneously does not entail a return to a social-democratic gradualist view, for this consciousness does not develop gradually, accumulating steadily and inevitably. On the contrary, it takes giant and sudden leaps forward and can suffer equally catastrophic shipwrecks. Nor does the consciousness spread evenly through the class, so the consciousness of the advanced socialist workers must be organised and centralised to increase to the maximum its influence within the ideologically heterogeneous class as a whole. These ideas will be returned to and developed later in this work, especially when dealing with the contribution of Rosa Luxemburg.

4. The Bolshevik-Menshevik split

Because of its great theoretical, historical and practical significance, *What is to be done?* tends to be regarded as the founding document of Bolshevism. In a certain sense this is correct, which is why we have subjected it to such detailed analysis. But it was not *What is to be done?* which directly occasioned the split of the Russian Social-Democratic Labour Party into Bolshevik and Menshevik factions. On the contrary, the pamphlet acted as a rallying point in the struggle for the second congress of the RSDLP, bringing together militants on an all-Russian basis and having the apparently united support of the leading intellectuals of Russian marxism—Plekhanov, Martov, Axelrod, Trotsky etc. It was the attempt to put the programme of *What is to be done?* into practice that produced the split. Those who thought themselves in agreement in theory found themselves in violent disagreement when those theories were translated into practical rules and decisions at the second congress in London in 1903.

The history of the development of the split is both complicated and obscure. A blow-by-blow account of the disputes at the congress is available in Lenin's *One Step Forward, Two Steps Back* written immediately after the split in 1904. Briefly what happened was this. The formerly united (and dominant) Iskraist tendency within the party divided over the formulation of Paragraph I of the Rules. Martov's formulation was as follows: 'A member of the Russian Social-Democratic Labour Party is one who accepts its programme, supports the Party financially, and renders it regular personal assistance under the direction of one of its organisations.' Whereas Lenin's draft read: 'A member of the Party is one who accepts its programme and who supports the Party both financially and by *personal participation in* one of the Party organisations.' [My emphasis—J.M.] On this question the Iskraists split into two definite factions. Plekhanov supported Lenin, but when it came to the vote Martov, with the aid of anti-centralist 'economist' elements still within the party, gained a majority. But with the secession of the *Rabocheye Dyelo* economists and the Bund at a later session, the majority passed to Lenin's faction, which enabled him to push through his slate of candidates for the *Iskra* editorial board. This replaced the old board of six (Plekhanov, Axelrod, Zasulich, Lenin, Martov, Potressov) with a board of three (Lenin, Plekhanov, Martov). Martov and his supporters refused to accept this decision and Martov resigned from *Iskra*. The terms Bolshevik and Menshevik (meaning 'majority' and 'minority') referred to the vote on the editorial board, but, because officially the two factions remained parts of the same party, the names stuck and have passed into history.

For the purpose of this study it is necessary to ask two questions. First, what were these disputes, seemingly a hairsplitting wrangle about words, really about? Secondly, what was the impact of the split on the developing Leninist theory of the party? To grasp the real meaning of any dispute in the marxist movement it is always necessary to see it in its context. 'Truth is concrete' as Lenin was so fond of saying. Writing in this vein we find Paul Frölich who sums up the situation as follows:

> In order to understand these debates, it is necessary to keep in mind the state of the social-democratic movement at that time, with its unstable and anarchical network of circles, and the conditions in which an illegal party organisation had to operate under absolutism. At the same time, it is necessary to understand that deep political antagonisms were coming to a head in the discussions on the statutes, antagonisms which were still only felt rather than clearly expressed in any single argument. Lenin sensed grave dangers ahead and wanted to ward them off by organising the party more tightly. He was aware of the tremendous tasks which the party would face in the approaching revolution, and wanted to forge it into a weapon of iron. And, finally, he recognised that he alone out of the whole *Iskra* group would be able to lead the party with the necessary

confidence and determination. The very impersonal and objective way in which he reached this conclusion explains his obstinacy on this question.

The wording of the two proposals for Paragraph I of the statutes gives hardly an inkling of the antagonism. It is certain that Martov wanted a party with ill-defined boundaries in accordance with the actual state of the movement, and with strong autonomy for the individual groups; a party of agitation which would broadly and loosely embrace everybody who called himself a socialist. Lenin, however, felt it was important to overcome the autonomy and the isolation of the local groups, and thus avoid the dangers inherent in their over-simplified and ossified ideas, not to speak of their backward political development. He wanted a firmly and tightly organised party which, as the vanguard of the class, would be closely connected with it, but at the same time clearly distinct from it.[36]

There was, however, another aspect of the debate which Lenin fastened on. There was a second possible interpretation of Martov's formulation; 'that a Party organisation [would be] *entitled to regard* as a party member anyone who renders it regular personal assistance under its direction' and 'that a committee would assign functions and watch over their fulfilment'. Lenin comments:

> Such special assignments will never, of course, be made to the *mass* of the workers, to the *thousands* of proletarians (of whom Comrade Axelrod and Comrade Martynov spoke)—they will frequently be given precisely to . . . professors . . . high school students . . . and revolutionary youth . . . In a word, Comrade Martov's formula will either remain a dead letter, an empty phrase, or it will be of benefit mainly and almost exclusively to 'intellectuals who are thoroughly imbued with bourgeois individualism' and do not wish to join an organisation. *In words*, Martov's formulation defends the interests of the broad strata of the proletariat, but *in fact* it serves the interests of the *bourgeois intellectuals*, who fight shy of proletarian discipline and organisation.[37]

Raya Dunayevskaya also focuses on this point as the central question in the dispute.

> The disciplining by the local was so crucial to Lenin's conception that it held primacy over verbal adherence to marxist theory, propagandising marxist views, and holding a membership card . . . Lenin insisted that the marxist intellectual needed the *ideological* discipline of the proletarians in the local because otherwise he was resisting not only local discipline but

also resisting being theoretically disciplined by the *economic content* of the Russian revolution.[38]

It was this softness towards the bourgeois intellectuals which was probably the main cause of Martovite hostility to Lenin (and this would fit very well the pattern of future Bolshevik-Menshevik differences). But to counter this particular deviation Lenin did not have to leave the ground of Kautskyite social-democratic orthodoxy. The organisational views of the Mensheviks could be taken together with those of Bernstein, Jaurès and the general opportunist trend in international social democracy,[39] and there was even a lengthy quotation from Kautsky himself to fit the bill.[40] What was crucial for the *development* of Lenin's thought—i.e. what enabled him to make a breakthrough into a new marxist approach to organisation—was the question of the distinction between the party of the class and the class itself, which Lenin was forced to clarify by the debate on the conditions of membership.

> The stronger our party organisations, consisting of *real* social-democrats, the less wavering and instability there is *within* the party, the broader, more varied, richer and more fruitful will be the party's influence on the elements of the working-class *masses surrounding* it and guided by it. *The party, as the vanguard of the working class, must not be confused, after all, with the entire class.* [my emphasis—J.M.][41]

It is this last sentence which signifies the break with Marx's concept of organisation in which the distinction between party and class remains blurred, and, more decisively, with the orthodox social-democratic conception of the party as *representing* the class. What renders this break permanent rather than temporary, and of universal rather than merely Russian, significance is that Lenin roots it not in practical necessities of secrecy (though these are of course not lost sight of) nor in an erroneous theory of the introduction of consciousness 'from the outside' but in the objective situation of the proletariat under capitalism:

> Precisely because there are differences in degree of consciousness and degree of activity, a distinction must be made in degree of proximity to the party . . . it would be . . . 'tailism' to think that the entire class, or almost the entire class, can ever rise, under capitalism, to the level of consciousness and activity of its vanguard, of its social-democratic party.[42]

Of great importance in this passage is the charge of 'tailism' directed at his opponents. 'Tailism' (from the Russian khvost=tail) is Lenin's figurative and polemical term for the 'fatalism' which was to prove the Achilles' heel of the Second International. Running like a red thread through *One Step Forward, Two Steps Back* is the contrast between the Bolshevik activist, revolutionary outlook on the world and the 'tailist' fatalist complacency of the Mensheviks. Nothing illustrates this better than one of the disputes with Trotsky.

> To the category of arguments, which inevitably crop up when attempts are made to justify Martov's formulation, belongs in particular, Comrade Trotsky's statement that 'opportunism is produced by more complex (or: is determined by deeper) causes than one or another clause in the Rules: it is brought about by the relative level of development of bourgeois democracy and the proletariat.' The point is not that clauses in the Rules may produce opportunism, but that with their help a more or a less trenchant weapon against opportunism can be forged. The deeper its causes, the more trenchant should this weapon be. Therefore, to *justify* a formulation which opens the door to opportunism on the grounds that opportunism has 'deep causes' is tailism of the first water.[43]

Trotsky analyses and explains a phenomenon and leaves it at that. Lenin accepts the explanation but wants to use it to do something about it.

3.
Lenin: From Russian Bolshevism to the Communist International

As we have shown, by 1904 Lenin had developed a number of ideas which constituted a definite advance on the generally accepted view of the party. Because of this, and because of the historical continuity of the Bolshevik faction from the 1903 split to the 1917 revolution, it has commonly been assumed that Lenin had had almost from the first his own clearly worked out theory of the party, quite distinct from that of social democracy in the West. But this is to make the mistake of reading back into the past ideas that only became clear much later. In reality Lenin, at this stage, was not aware that he diverged in any fundamental way from social-democratic orthodoxy. He identified the Mensheviks with Bernsteinian 'revisionism' and himself with the mainstream Bebel-Kautsky tendency of the SPD.

The citations of Kautsky as *the* marxist authority are legion in Lenin's works at this time and remain so throughout the pre-war period. Even Kautsky's tendency to favour the Mensheviks is not allowed to affect this judgement; it is always attributed to Kautsky's ignorance of the real situation in Russia.[1] As late as August 1913 Lenin can refer to Bebel as a 'model workers' leader',[2] and praise him as the elaborator of 'the fundamentals of parliamentary tactics for German (and international) Social Democracy, tactics that never yield an inch to the enemy . . . (and are) always directed to the accomplishment of the final aim'.[3] As far as perceiving the conservatism of the SPD is concerned, not only Luxemburg, who saw its leaders at first hand, but also Trotsky were far in advance of Lenin. As early as 1906 Trotsky warned that:

The European socialist parties, particularly the largest of them, the German Social-Democratic Party, have developed their conservatism in proportion as the masses have embraced socialism and the more these masses have become organised and disciplined. As a consequence of this social democracy as an organisation embodying the political experience of the proletariat may at a certain moment become a direct obstacle to open conflict between the workers and bourgeois reaction.[4]

This point is stressed as a corrective to the widespread tendency to exaggerate the 'unity' of Lenin's thought, to make of his ideas a totally consistent system in which everything from beginning to end fits neatly into place.[5] As Trotsky once commented: 'If Lenin in 1903 had under-stood and formulated everything that was required for the coming times, then the remainder of his life would have consisted only of reiterations. In reality this was not at all the case.'[6] There is a great gap between Lenin's theory of the party in 1903–04 and that of 1919 at the founding of the Communist International. Lenin developed that theory, not all at once, but through a series of responses to and generalisations from the course of the class struggle. Consequently, as with Marx, an understand-ing of that theory cannot be extracted from one or two key texts, but must be drawn from an examination of Lenin's practice as a whole.

1. The impact of 1905

After the 1903 split, the next event which had a major impact on Lenin's theory of the party was the 1905 revolution. The first effect of 1905 was to deepen the split between the Bolsheviks and the Mensheviks. Originally the division had been only about organisation, apparently unrelated to questions of programme or strategy, but now a fundamental divergence emerged in the estimation of the driving forces of the revolution. Lenin, as we have indicated above, accepted the bourgeois nature of the revolution, but, because of the conservative, weak and cowardly nature of the Russian bourgeoisie, held that the bourgeois revolution would have to be made by the proletariat in alliance with the peasantry. Attempting to concretise this position for the purpose of revolutionary action, Lenin argued that the social democrats should work to break the influence of the bourgeois liberals (Cadets etc.) on the peasantry, and then stage a joint proletarian-peasant insurrection to overthrow the autocracy. Issuing from a successful rising would be a provisional revolutionary government consisting of the revolutionary workers' party (the Social

Democrats) and the party of the revolutionary peasantry (the Socialist Revolutionaries) which would represent the 'democratic dictatorship of the proletariat and the peasantry'. After a brief period of energetic measures to sweep away every vestige of feudalism, the provisional revolutionary government would summon a constituent assembly, which because of the peasant majority of the population would inevitably be anti-socialist, and the social democrats would then become an opposition party leading the struggle for socialism. In this way, maintained Lenin, the Russian revolution would be thoroughgoing (like the great French Revolution, rather than a shabby compromise like Germany in 1848) and would secure the best possible conditions for the future battles of the proletariat.[7]

The Mensheviks however rejected this perspective. More and more they tended towards the view that because the revolution was bourgeois its driving force must be the bourgeoisie, with only a subsidiary role assigned to the proletariat. The job of social democrats was to pressurise the bourgeois liberals so as to 'revolutionise' them, but at the same time not to frighten them. They rejected the formula of 'democratic dictatorship of the proletariat and the peasantry', and participation in a provisional revolutionary government as likely to 'cause the bourgeois classes to recoil from the revolution and thus diminish its sweep'.[8] During the rise of the revolution, the Mensheviks were in large part swept along by events, but as soon as the movement began to ebb they more and more came to express regret at the extreme positions and actions into which they had been pushed—a process which culminated in Plekhanov's notorious remark, 'We should not have taken up arms.'[9]

Lenin's observation of the conduct of the Mensheviks convinced him of the connection between opportunism in organisation and opportunism in politics. Thus, although the joint action of Bolshevik and Menshevik workers in the revolutionary struggles produced great pressures for unification to which Lenin formally acceded, he became more determined than ever to strengthen the independent organisation of his own tendency. In his article of 1910 on 'The historical meaning of the inner-party struggle in Russia', it is on the issue of the role of the proletariat in the revolution that Lenin focuses, writing that 'Bolshevism as a tendency took definite shape in the spring and summer of 1905'.[10]

The second effect of the revolution was to bring about a shift of emphasis in Lenin's conception of the relationship between party and class. In *What is to be done?* Lenin had justified his view of the party with the argument that socialism had to be introduced into the working class 'from without', and that spontaneously the working class could not rise above the level of trade unionism. In the face of the enormous and spontaneous revolutionary achievements of the Russian working class, the tone of Lenin's writings changes completely.

> There is not the slightest doubt that the revolution will teach social-democratism to the masses of the workers in Russia . . . At such a time the working class feels an instinctive urge for open revolutionary action.[11]
> The working class is instinctively, spontaneously social-democratic.[12]

It is now that Lenin notes 'how the elementary instinct of the working-class movement is able to correct the conceptions of the greatest minds'[13] and from this point on he becomes circumspect about the formulations of *What is to be done?* '*What is to be done?*', he writes in 1907, 'is a controversial correction of "economist" distortions and it would be wrong to regard the pamphlet in any other light'.[14] This reappraisal did not, however, involve a return to a spontaneist or fatalist attitude to the tasks of the party—on the contrary it was precisely on this score that Lenin most strongly attacked the Mensheviks. 'Good marchers, but bad leaders, they belittle the materialist conception of history by ignoring the active, leading and guiding part in history which can and must be played by parties that understand the material prerequisites of a revolution and that have placed themselves at the head of the progressive classes.'[15] The break with economistic fatalism that was achieved in *What is to be done?* and *One Step Forward, Two Steps Back* is maintained and developed, but freed of the elitist foundation that Lenin had at first given it. The formulations in *Two Tactics* are eminently dialectical. 'Undoubtedly, the revolution will teach us, and will teach the masses of the people. But the question that now confronts a militant political party is: shall we be able to teach the revolution anything?'[16]

The corollary of this theoretical shift was a struggle by Lenin within the Bolshevik faction against the influence of the 'professional revolutionaries' or 'committeemen' on whom he had placed so much emphasis a year or two earlier. In the pre-revolutionary period of clandestine activity these 'committeemen' provided the stability and the expertise necessary to firmly establish the party in such difficult circumstances, but they also became prey to a certain routinism which revealed its reactionary features with the arrival of the revolution. In particular they were the tangible embodiment of the theory of 'bringing socialism to the working class from without', and as such tended to have a superior attitude towards the workers, with the result that there were practically no workers on the Bolshevik committees. The question of bringing workers onto the committees came up at the Bolsheviks' third congress in April 1905. Krupskaya has described the debate:

> Vladimir Ilyich vigorously defended the idea of including workers. The people abroad, Bogdanov and the writers were also in favour. The Komitetchiks (committeemen) were against. Both sides became very heated . . .
>
> In his speech in this discussion Vladimir Ilyich said: 'I think we should consider the question more broadly. To bring workers on to the committees is not only an educational but a political task. The workers have a class instinct, and even with little political experience they quite quickly become steadfast Social Democrats. I would very much like to see eight workers on our committees for every two intellectuals . . . '
>
> When Mikhailov (Pestolovsky) said, 'so in practical work very small demands are made of intellectuals, but extremely big demands are made of workers', Vladimir Ilyich cried out: 'That is absolutely true!' His exclamation was drowned in a chorus of—'Not true!' from the Komitetchiks. When Rumyanstiev said 'There is only one worker on the Petersburg committee, although work has been going on there for fifteen years' Vladimir Ilyich shouted: 'What a disgrace'.[17]

The debate about worker involvement on the committees, over which, incidentally, Lenin was defeated by the congress, was only one aspect of Lenin's fight against conservative sectarianism in the Bolshevik ranks. Another issue over which he clashed with his supporters was the attitude of the party to the soviet. Trotsky, the soviet's chairman, has described the initial response of the Bolsheviks to this historic organisation.

> The Petersburg Committee of the Bolsheviks was frightened at first by such an innovation as a non-partisan representation of the embattled masses, and could find nothing better to do than to present the soviet with an ultimatum: immediately adopt a Social-Democratic programme, or disband. The Petersburg soviet as a whole, including the contingent of Bolshevik workingmen as well, ignored this ultimatum without batting an eyelash.[18]

Even from abroad Lenin saw the sterility of this approach and opposed it in a letter to the party's paper *Novaya Zhizn*, in which he argued that it was not a question of the soviet *or* the party, but of '*both* the Soviet of Workers' Deputies *and* the party',[19] and that it would be inadvisable for the soviet 'to adhere wholly to any one party'.[20] 'To my mind', wrote Lenin, 'the Soviet of Workers' Deputies, as a revolutionary centre providing political leadership, is not too broad an organisation but on the contrary, a much too narrow one. The soviet must proclaim itself the provisional revolutionary government, or form such a government.'[21]

The essential difference between the 'committeemen' and Lenin was that the former wished to apply in the revolution the concept of the party which had operated in the pre-revolutionary period, whereas Lenin wanted to completely re-organise the party so as to embrace the new forces and confront the new tasks thrown up by the revolution.

> If we fail to show bold initiative in setting up new organisations, we shall have to give up as groundless all pretensions to the role of vanguard. If we stop helplessly at the achieved boundaries, forms and confines of the committees, groups, meetings, and circles, we shall merely prove our own incapacity. Thousands of circles are now springing up everywhere without our aid, without any definite programme or aim, simply under the impact of events . . . Let all such circles, except those that are avowedly non-social-democratic, either directly join the party or *align themselves with the party*. In the latter event we must not demand that they accept our programme or that they necessarily enter into organisational relations with us. Their mood of protest and their sympathy for the cause of international revolutionary social democracy in themselves suffice, provided the social democrats work effectively among them.[22]

The party machine resisted Lenin's exhortations but the course of events was on his side. By November 1905 he could note with satisfaction:

> At the third congress of the Party I suggested that there be about eight workers to every two intellectuals in the party committees. How obsolete that suggestion seems today! Now we must wish for the new party organisations to have one social-democratic intellectual to several hundred social-democratic workers.[23]

Just as Lenin's theoretical reappraisal of the spontaneous capacities of the proletariat did not involve a return to economic fatalism, neither did his new views on party organisation mean adoption of the Menshevik position of the broad party. The open-ended expansion envisaged by Lenin *in the revolutionary period* was possible *only* on the basis of the solid preparation of the party beforehand.

> Is social democracy endangered by the realisation of the plan we propose?
>
> Danger may be said to lie in a sudden influx of large numbers of non-social-democrats into the party. If that occurred, the party would be dissolved among the masses, it would cease to be the conscious vanguard of its class, its role would be reduced to that of a tail. That would mean a very deplorable period indeed. And this danger *could* undoubtedly become a *very serious* one *if* we showed any inclination towards demagogy, if we lacked party principles . . . entirely, or if those principles were feeble and shaky. But the fact is that no such 'ifs' exist. We Bolsheviks have never shown any inclination towards demagogy . . . We have demanded class consciousness from those joining the party, we have insisted on the tremendous importance of continuity in the party's development, we have preached discipline and demanded that *every* party member be trained in one or other of the party organisations . . .
>
> Don't forget that in every live and growing party there will always be elements of instability, vacillation, wavering. But these elements can be influenced, and they will submit to the influence of the steadfast and solid core of social democrats.[24]

Thus the experience of the 'great dress rehearsal' of the Russian Revolution raised Lenin's theory of the party to a new level. It deepened his opposition to opportunism and strengthened his determination to build a specifically *revolutionary* party. It also clarified his understanding of the relationship between party and class. The party remains a vanguard, distinct from the class as a whole, but now it is the party of the advanced workers—a part of the class, not the party of the declassed intelligentsia introducing socialism 'from without'. But it was not only the upsurge of revolution that affected Lenin, the period of reaction which followed also added important elements to his theory of the party.

2. Reaction steels

After the defeat of the 1905 revolution terrible reaction engulfed Russia for a number of years. Demoralisation set in all round and the Bolshevik organisations were shattered.

It is interesting to compare Lenin's response to this situation with that of Marx after the defeat of the 1848 revolutions. Marx dissolved the Communist League, left the emigres to their squabbles, and retired to the study. Lenin, however, clung desperately both to the remnants of his party organisation and to the *party* idea, defending them passionately against all assaults. 'Let the Black-Hundred diehards rejoice and howl' he wrote, 'let the reaction rage . . . A party which succeeds in consolidating itself for persistent work in contact with the masses, a party of the advanced class which succeeds in organising its vanguard and which directs its forces in such a way as to influence in a social-democratic spirit every sign of life of the proletariat—such a party will win no matter what happens.'[25]

To preserve and build the kind of party he wanted Lenin had to fight many factional battles. The three most important of these were against (a) right wing 'liquidationism', (b) ultra-left 'otzovism' ('recallism') and (c) centrist 'conciliationism'. These disputes became very fierce and very tangled, and the theoretical level of the polemics which they produced was not always very high. Consequently there is no need to go into detail about them here, but nonetheless certain important general principles emerged which are worthy of note, and which stood Lenin in good stead in later years.[26] Firstly, that the party is not only an organisation for attack, but also for 'retreat in good order'. 'Of all the defeated opposition and revolutionary parties, the Bolsheviks effected the most orderly retreat, with the least loss to their "army", with its core best preserved.'[27] Secondly, the principle of 'combining illegal work with the utilisation of "legal opportunities"'.[28] And thirdly, the principle of carrying the fight against opportunism through to its organisational conclusions, and effecting a split with all non-revolutionary elements.

It was this last point which was really the distinct hallmark of Leninism, and which resulted in 1912 in the formal foundation of the Russian Social-Democratic Labour Party (Bolsheviks) as a completely separate and independent party. Kautsky had fought Bernstein theoretically, but the revisionists were not expelled from the SPD. Rosa Luxemburg fought Kautsky and the SPD centre, but built no separate organisation. Trotsky was opposed to both liquidationism and otzovism and was just as critical as Lenin of the political line of the Mensheviks,[29] and yet he actively worked against a split. It was also an advance on Lenin's own earlier position, in that the 1903 split had in large part been the work of the Mensheviks, and Lenin had frequently been willing to countenance reunification, whereas now he broke with the Mensheviks once and for all.

The result of Lenin's determined struggles during the reaction was that the Bolsheviks started life as a fully independent party just as the working-class movement began to get going again. The slowly reviving movement received a great impetus from the massacre of gold miners in Lena on 4 April 1912, which produced a wave of strikes, protest meetings and demonstrations throughout the country, culminating in a 400,000 strong May Day strike. Lenin intervened in this situation through the production of a legal daily newspaper, *Pravda*, the first issue of which appeared 18 days after the Lena massacre. *Pravda* combined an intransigent revolutionary political line[30] with numerous reports from workers themselves chronicling their everyday conditions and struggles. In one year 11,000 such workers' letters and contributions were published.[31] The daily circulation of *Pravda* reached over 40,000 and the formation of workers' groups to collect money for the paper compensated for the lack of a mass legal party. On the basis of a painstaking analysis of these collections Lenin showed that the Bolsheviks had won clear hegemony over the politically conscious workers. In 1913 *Pravda* received donations from 2,181 groups, while the Menshevik papers got donations from 661 groups. In 1914 up to 13 May the figure for donations to *Pravda* was 2,873, as against 671 for the Mensheviks.[32] From this Lenin concluded, 'Pravdism, Pravdist decisions and Pravdist tactics have united four-fifths of Russia's class-conscious workers.'[33] Lenin had thus become the first marxist to have created a party consisting solely of revolutionaries, without any reformist or opportunist wing, which also had a substantial base in the working class.

3. The most revolutionary section of the Second International

At this point it is useful to examine what the Bolshevik party, the tangible embodiment of Lenin's ideas on the party, actually looked like in practice and see how it compared with the more 'orthodox' social-democratic parties.

Firstly, the Bolsheviks were, of course, an illegal party operating in a country where there were no democratic liberties and no effective trade unions, whereas most Western social democracies had long since obtained their legality. Consequently the Bolsheviks did not and could not develop, as did for example the SPD, a broad layer of functionaries consisting of local officials, trade-union leaders, members of parliament, local councillors etc. This is a stratum which is inevitably subject to enormous 'moderating' pressures from its environment. Raised to a privileged position vis-à-vis the rank-and-file workers, such functionaries find that there is a definite role for them to play, not only within the workers' movement, but also within capitalism, as mediators between the classes, and therefore they have a direct interest in social peace. They thus constitute a major conservative force. Within international social democracy this stratum acted as a permanent base for reformism. The fact that the Bolshevik leadership and its local cadre were closer to the prison cell or Siberian exile than they were to ministerial posts or to trade-union officialdom, and that the party itself had no more than a threadbare administrative apparatus, made the party relatively (though not absolutely) immune to bureaucratic routinism.

Secondly, the Bolshevik party was heavily proletarian in composition. David Lane has produced the following breakdown of Bolshevik membership for 1905: workers, 61.9 per cent; peasants, 4.8 per cent; white collar, 27.4 per cent; others 5.9 per cent;[34] and concludes, 'if judged by the bottom levels of the party and particularly by its popular support, it may be said that the Bolsheviks were a "workers" party', whereas, 'it seems probable that the Mensheviks had comparatively more "petty-bourgeois" members, and fewer working-class supporters at the lower levels'.[35] During the reaction there was a mass exodus of intellectuals from the movement, whereas the factory cells, albeit isolated, survived better, thus increasing the party's proletarianisation. Lenin's above-mentioned analysis of money collections between 1912 and 1914 confirms this picture. Of all the donations to *Pravda* in the first quarter of 1914, 87 per cent came from workers' collections and 13 per cent from non-workers, whereas only 44 per cent of donations to the Menshevik papers came from workers and 56 per cent from non-workers.[36]

The combination of the illegal status of the party and its proletarian composition made for an organisational structure radically different from the normal social-democratic tradition. Despite their revolutionary rhetoric, the essential strategy of most of the parties of the Second International was the achievement of the parliamentary majority. Consequently the base units of these parties were organised on residential or geographical lines, so as to facilitate mobilisation of the party membership for electoral campaigns in the respective electoral districts. In Russia the absence of parliamentary elections (such elections as did take place to the Duma were on a factory basis) and the need for secrecy led the Bolsheviks to base their organisation on the factories. Osip Piatnitsky, an old Bolshevik organisation man, records that 'during all periods the lower party organisation of the Bolsheviks existed at the place of work rather than at the place of residence'.[37] This structure, despite the smallness of the Bolshevik party, made for a more intimate relationship between the party and the proletariat than was achieved by the social-democratic parties, where contact with the factories tended to be maintained only indirectly through control of the trade-unions, and where a certain division of labour operated between the industrial struggle handled by the unions and the political struggle handled by the party. No such de facto separation occurred with the Bolsheviks. Piatnitsky has described the work of Bolshevik factory cells:

> In Czarist Russia the cells . . . utilised all the grievances in the factories; the gruffness of the foremen, deductions from wages, fines, the failure to provide medical aid in accidents, etc, for oral agitation at the bench, through leaflets, meetings at the factory gates or in the factory yards, and separate meetings of the more class-conscious and revolutionary workers. The Bolsheviks always showed the connection between the maltreatment of factories, and the rule of the autocracy . . . At the same time the autocracy was connected up in the agitation of the party cells with the capitalist system, so that at the very beginning of the development of the labour movement the Bolsheviks established a connection between the economic struggle and the political.[38]

Thus the Bolshevik party, rather than being simply the political representative of the working class, was an interventionist combat party striving to lead and guide the class in all its battles.

Also important was the youth of the party membership. In 1907 approximately 22 per cent of the party members were less than 20 years old; 37 per cent were between 20 and 24, and 16 per cent between 25 and 29.[39] Trotsky has commented on the significance of this. 'Bolshevism when underground was always a party of young workers. The Mensheviks relied upon the more respectable skilled upper stratum, always prided themselves on it, and looked down on the Bolsheviks. Subsequent events harshly showed them their mistake. At the decisive moment the youth carried with them the more mature stratum and even the old folks.'[40] And Lane notes that 'the Bolsheviks were younger than the Mensheviks at the lowest levels of party organisation and more so among the "activists" than among the ordinary members. This suggests that the Bolshevik organisational structure allowed the young to advance to positions of responsibility more easily than did the Menshevik . . . Politically, these young men may have provided more dynamic and vigorous leadership for the Bolshevik faction.'[41] Certainly the youth of the party was another major factor in freeing it from conservative routinism.

Finally, the Bolshevik party was a disciplined body. The internal regime of the party was characterised as democratic centralism, but this phrase in itself does not have great significance. As an organisational formula it was not at all specifically Leninist, being accepted in theory by both the Mensheviks and many other social-democratic parties.[42] What mattered was the interpretation given to democratic centralism in practice. Lenin defined it as 'unity of action, freedom of discussion and criticism',[43] by which he meant freedom of criticism within the bounds of the party programme and until a definite decision was reached, then the implementation of that decision by the party as one. No party which contains both a revolutionary and a reformist wing, i.e. groups with fundamentally divergent aims, can in practice be a disciplined organisation. Thus although German Social Democracy attached great importance to administrative centralisation and party unity, it had a very lax attitude to breaches of discipline by party dignitaries, trade-union leaders and so on. Discipline exists to achieve unity in action, but if organisational unity is placed above principle, then real discipline inevitably disappears. 'Unless the masses are organised', wrote Lenin, 'the proletariat is nothing. Organised—it is everything. Organisation means unity of action, unity in practical operations. But every action is valuable, of course, only because and insofar as it serves to push things forward and not backward . . . Organisation not based on principle is meaningless, and in practice converts the workers into a miserable appendage of the bourgeoisie in power . . . Therefore class-conscious workers must never forget that serious violations of principle occur which make the severance of all organisational relations imperative.'[44]

The Bolshevik party was compelled by its situation to be disciplined, and it was able to achieve the necessary discipline because it was politically united. But it is important to realise that this discipline did not, as was often claimed, rule out independent initiative from the rank-and-file of the party. The same repressive conditions which made unity in action a necessity also compelled the local sections of the party to act for themselves. Piatnitsky writes:

> The initiative of the local party organisations, of the cells, was encouraged. Were the Bolsheviks of Odessa, or Moscow, or Baku, or Tiflis, always to have waited for the directives from the Central Committee, the provincial committees, etc. which during the years of the reaction and of the war frequently did not exist at all owing to arrests, what would have been the result? The Bolsheviks would not have captured the working masses and exercised any influence over them.[45]

All these factors combined made Lenin's Bolshevik party, on the eve of the first world war, in the words of Trotsky, 'the most revolutionary—indeed, the only revolutionary—section of the Second International'.[46]

4. The break with social democracy

Trotsky's characterisation of the Bolsheviks as 'the only revolutionary section of the Second International', however, also indicates the limits of Lenin's achievements up to this point, for it makes clear the fact that the Bolsheviks remained *a section* of social democracy. This in itself shows that although Lenin had developed in practice a party quite at variance with the social-democratic norm, he had not yet consciously generalised this experience into a distinct and new theory of the party. It was only the collapse of the International in the face of the world war that brought about Lenin's complete theoretical break with the old socialism and the birth of a specifically Leninist *theory* of the party.

Lenin, it is well known, was taken completely by surprise by the support given to the war by all the main European socialist parties, in total defiance of all their past policy. His first reaction to the issue of *Vorwärts* recording the SPD's vote for war credits was that it must be a forgery. But once he had grasped the scale of the capitulation his thought developed extremely rapidly. Lenin's very first article after the outbreak of the war, 'The Tasks of Revolutionary Social Democracy in the European War', written not later than 28 August 1914, not only condemned the leaders of international social democracy for their 'betrayal of socialism'[47] and recorded the 'ideological and political bankruptcy of the International',[48] but also identified in this betrayal and abandonment of past positions a *continuation* of tendencies long at work in the pre-war period. Social-chauvinism is identified as the product and development of opportunism. 'This collapse [of the International] has been mainly caused by the actual prevalance in it of petty-bourgeois opportunism . . . The so-called Centre of the German and other social-democratic parties has in actual fact faintheartedly capitulated to the opportunists.'[49] From this Lenin immediately drew the conclusion that 'it must be the task of the future International resolutely and irrevocably to rid itself of this bourgeois trend in socialism'.[50]

From this point on Lenin would have no truck with schemes to reunite or resurrect the old International. 'On the contrary, this collapse must be frankly recognised and understood, so as to make it possible to build up a new and more lasting socialist unity of the workers of all countries.'[51] By 1 November the Bolshevik Central Committee had issued the slogan 'Long live a proletarian International freed from opportunism'.[52] In December Lenin was asking 'is it not better to give up the name of Social Democrats, which has been besmirched and degraded by them, and return to the old marxist name of Communists?'[53] and by February 1915 the Bolshevik party conference had committed itself officially to the eventual creation of a 'Third International'.[54]

Up till 1914 Lenin had seen himself as an orthodox social democrat applying to the peculiar conditions of Tsarist Russia the tried and tested theory and method of Kautsky and Bebel. But the decision in favour of a Third International signified not a determination to uphold that tradition, abandoned by its leaders, but a thorough-going rejection of it. Lenin levelled two interconnected charges at the Second International: a) that it was the product of a prolonged period of 'peace'—'peace' signifying not only peace between nations but also relative peace between classes—in which it had become so accustomed to legal methods and the growth of its legal mass-organisations that it was unwilling and unable to make the necessary transition to illegal work; and b) that it was a coalition between revolutionaries and opportunists to the advantage of the latter.

Typical of the socialist parties of the epoch of the Second International was one that tolerated in its midst an opportunism built up in decades of the 'peaceful' period . . . This type has out-lived itself. If the war ends in 1915, will any thinking socialist be found willing to begin, in 1916, restoring the workers' parties *together* with the opportunists, knowing from experience that in any new crisis all of them *to a man* . . . will be for the bourgeoisie.[55]

Compared with the Second International, which Kautsky aptly described as 'an instrument for peace, unsuitable for war', the Third International was to be precisely an instrument of war—international civil war against the imperialist bourgeoisie—and therefore could tolerate in its ranks neither a fifth column nor waverers. In mounting this critique of social democracy it is clear that Lenin based his ideas on his experiences with the Bolsheviks and the struggle against Menshevism, but now for the first time these experiences and the numerous theoretical insights that accompanied them were generalised internationally into a new theory of the party to replace everywhere the old forms of organisation.

A new theory of the party, however, could not stand on its own; it required the all-round regeneration of marxism. For a theory of the party is merely the application to organisation of an analysis of the class struggle as a whole. The social-democratic parties were both producer and product of a mechanistic and fatalist interpretation of marxism in which the unification of the proletariat and the growth of its political party were seen as proceeding smoothly and harmoniously in a steadily ascending line as an inevitable consequence of capitalist development. The tasks of marxists in this scheme were formulated by Kautsky as 'building up the organisation, winning all positions of power, which we are able to win and hold securely by our own strength, studying the state and society and educating the masses; other aims we cannot consciously and systematically set either to ourselves or to our organisations',[56] and the object as 'the conquest of state power by winning a majority in parliament and by raising parliament to the rank of master of the government'.[57] The latter would inevitably be realised provided only that the party avoided the disruption of its prized 'organisations' through being drawn into foolish or premature conflicts. In practice the avoidance of such upsets became the main preoccupation of many of the social-democratic leaders. In the first years of the war Lenin set about systematically dismantling this perspective and establishing a new theoretical foundation for the future Third International. This project led Lenin into three main areas of theoretical investigation: (a) philosophy (b) economics (the analysis of imperialism) (c) politics (the state). Each of these had an important bearing on his theory of the party, and therefore, although it is not possible here to go deeply into any of these questions, it is necessary at least to indicate the main interconnections.

In relation to philosophy we have already argued that the key to Lenin's attitude in the original split with the Mensheviks was his rejection of the latter's fatalist ('tailist') approach to problems of organisation. At that time, Lenin's position was the product more of his keen political instinct and practical judgement than of a philosophical break with mechanical materialism, as is illustrated by his formulations in 'Materialism and Empirio-Criticism'.[58] At the end of 1914, however, Lenin plunged into the study of Hegel, in particular Hegel's *Science of Logic*. Lenin, like Marx, never wrote his 'Dialectics', but nonetheless his marginal notes on Hegel[59] show clearly the philosophical 'revolution' brought about by this reading. For the first time Lenin grasps clearly and assimilates the marxian dialectics. Through the restoration of these dialectics and of practice to their rightful place in the marxist world view,[60] Lenin established the philosophical basis for a party which aimed not passively to reflect the working class and await the working out of iron historical laws, but actually to intervene in the shaping of history.

In relation to economics, Lenin's task was to show that the objective situation was ripe for the creation of a new international party which was revolutionary not only in its ultimate aims but also in its immediate advocacy and preparation of revolutionary methods of struggle.

In his booklet *Imperialism, the Highest Stage of Capitalism*, Lenin aimed to show that on a *world* scale revolution was on the order of the day. Lenin's argument, in its bare bones, was that imperialism was the product of the transformation, through the law of concentration of capital, of capitalism based on free competition into its opposite, monopoly capitalism. This was accompanied by the dominance of finance capital over industrial capital, and the accumulation of a surplus of capital which could only find profitable outlets in the backward countries where labour was cheap and capital scarce. Consequently the world had been divided up between the great monopolies and their respective 'home' governments. Since such division could take place only on the basis of relative strength, and since the relative strengths of the monopolies and the capitalist powers would not remain stable, so struggle for redivision, again on the basis of strength (i.e. war), would inevitably set in. On this basis any achievement of peace would merely be the prelude to a new war. Above all imperialism aggravated the contradiction between the socialisation of production and its private appropriation; and thus imperialism marked the beginning of the decline of capitalism and the opening of the era of 'wars and revolutions'.

In addition to establishing the objective basis for a new revolutionary international, Lenin's analysis of imperialism also provided an economic foundation for his critique of the Second International. Recalling Engel's comments on the bourgeoisification of a section of the English proletariat due to England's industrial and colonial monopoly,[61] Lenin argued that imperialist monopolies gained 'superprofits' from their exploitation of the colonies and that this enabled 'the bourgeoisie of an imperialist "Great" Power [to] *economically bribe* the upper strata of "its" workers'.[62] In the nineteenth century this had been possible only in England, but it had operated there for decades to corrupt the labour movement. Now on the other hand '*every* imperialist "Great" Power can and does bribe *smaller* strata [than in England in 1848–68] of the "labour aristocracy"'.[63] In this way 'in all countries the bourgeoisie has already . . . secured for itself "bourgeois labour parties" of social chauvinists'.[64] Thus Lenin established that opportunism, or reformism, in the working-class movement was not just an alternative school of thought, a sign of immaturity or even simply a product of the pressure of bourgeois ideology; rather it was 'substantiated economically'.[65] Opportunism was the sacrifice of the overall interests of the proletariat as a whole for the immediate interests of separate groups of workers. The concept of the 'bourgeois labour party' signifies that opportunism is regarded as the agent of the class enemy within the ranks of the proletariat.

This definition of opportunism, which no marxist had formulated so clearly before, is crucial for Lenin's theory of the party. It is the basic reason why the party must strictly exclude all reformist trends from its ranks. It is a recognition that the revolutionary party must be organised for struggle not only against the bourgeoisie, but also (in a different way) against bourgeois organisations within the working class. It is an understanding and materialist explanation of the difficulties involved in the transition from the class-in-itself to the class-for-itself. In 1901 Lenin had grasped this problem but had explained it in terms of the inability of the working class to achieve socialist consciousness by its own efforts. Now he explained it in terms of the contradiction between the historical and immediate interests of the proletariat, which for *limited periods* and *limited strata* could predominate over the ultimate need for class unity. The socialist unification of the working class develops dialectically, through internal struggle. As the agent of this struggle, the revolutionary party must confine its membership to those for whom the overall interests of the proletariat stand higher than immediate interests, in a word, to internationalists.

Finally there is the question of the state, which was brought to the fore by the debates on imperialism and the war.[66] The essence of socialist revolution is the transfer of state power from the bourgeoisie to the proletariat. Since the organisation of the party is necessarily in part determined by the tasks it will have to perform in the revolution, how this transfer of power is envisaged is of great importance to the theory of the party. The theorists of the Second International did not rule out violence, particularly defensive violence, in the struggle for power, but essentially they expected the revolution to leave the state machine itself intact. The role of the party would be to take over the existing state, no doubt changing its leading personnel, reorganising it and so on, but not fundamentally challenging its structure. With such a view of the tasks of the revolution in regard to the state, the centre of gravity of the class struggle must inevitably be seen as being in parliament and parliamentary elections. Thus Kautsky wrote—'This direct action of the unions can operate effectively only as an auxiliary and reinforcement to, and not as substitute for, parliamentary action',[67] and '[parliament] is the most powerful lever that can be used to raise the proletariat out of its economic, social and moral degradation'.[68] From this it follows that the leadership of the party comes to lie with its parliamentary representatives, since it is through a parliamentary majority that the revolutionary government will be formed. In this conception the role of the rank-and-file of the party, and even more so that of workers outside the party, is essentially passive: for even though they may be called upon to fight, they are not expected either to create new structures of power themselves or to participate in running them. Social democracy's bureaucratic conception of the revolution entailed a bureaucratic organisation of the party.

For the Bolsheviks, as we have shown above, none of this has applied because no modern 'democratic' state existed in Russia and they had from the start been illegal. But now, with a new International in mind, Lenin had to confront this problem theoretically. The result was that he rediscovered, clarified and systematised Marx's generalisation from the experience of the French revolutions of 1848–52 and 1871 that 'the working class cannot simply lay hold of the ready-made state machinery, and wield it for its own purposes'.[69] Lenin, in his notebooks, summed up the question as follows:

> Changes after 1871? They are all such, or their general nature or their sum is such, that bureaucracy has everywhere soared (both in parliamentarism, within it—in local self-government, in the joint-stock companies, in the trust and so on). That is the first thing. And second: the workers' 'socialist' parties have, by ¾, 'grown into' a *similar* bureaucracy. The split between the social-patriots and the internationalists, between the reformists and the revolutionaries, has, consequently, a still more profound significance: the reformists and the social-patriots 'perfect' the bureaucratic-state machine . . . while the revolutionaries must *'smash'* it, this 'bureaucratic-military state machine', smash it, replacing it by the 'Commune', a new 'semi-state'.
>
> One could, probably, in brief and drastically, express the whole matter thus; *replacement* of the old ('ready-made') state machine *and parliaments* by *Soviets of Workers' Deputies* and their trustees. Therein lies the essence!![70]

A party aiming to smash the state cannot be organised in the same way as a party intending to take it over. Its centre of gravity must be not in parliament, but in factories, from which the new state will issue. The rank-and-file of the party cannot simply be passive voters or even propagandists. They themselves have to become leaders of their fellow workers, builders of their own new state machine. Moreover, the thesis that the bourgeois state had to be smashed, finally closed the option of a peaceful or constitutional revolution even for the 'freest' of democratic republics.[71] Proletarian revolution would by definition involve a mass struggle for power, and therefore every revolutionary party would have to be so organised as to be able to lead such a struggle. This meant the creation of parallel legal and illegal apparatuses, the organisation of fighting detachments, the creation of party groups within the armed forces and so on.

Finally, Lenin's theory of the state radically altered current conceptions of the relationship of the party to the workers' state during and after the conquest of power. If the revolution means the taking over of the existing state, then the class content of the state as a workers' state is defined by the party that controls it. The party and the state must merge. In this sense, for social democracy, the party was the embryo of the new state. Lenin's theory of the replacement of the existing state by soviets (workers' councils) established a clear distinction between the workers' state and the revolutionary party. The class content of the new state is defined by the fact that it is the creation of the working class as a whole, and involves the class as a whole in its operation. 'Under socialism . . . the *mass* of the population will rise to taking an *independent* part, not only in voting and elections, *but also in the everyday administration* of *the state*.'[72] The role of the party is not to *be* the workers' state, but to be the advanced minority which leads and guides the process of the new state's creation and consolidation. As Chris Harman has put it, 'The Soviet state is the highest concrete embodiment of the self-activity of the whole working class; the party is that section of the class that is most conscious of the world historical implications of self-activity.'[73] It is because the party and the state are not identical that more than one party can contend for influence and government within the framework of the institutions of workers' state power.

Thus Lenin's theory of the state was an indispensable compliment to his theory of the party. It was this that ensured that the restriction of the party to the advanced minority of the proletariat in no way implied the party substituting itself for the class as a whole or attempting to seize power as a minority. It was the theory of the state that brought the Leninist theory of the party into harmony with the fundamental principle of marxism that 'the emancipation of the working class must be conquered by the working class itself'.[74]

As a result of these few years of intense theoretical labour, the theoretical foundations of the Second International had been completely demolished and Lenin's new theory of the party was now fully formed (which is not to say that further additions or developments were excluded). The new theory represented not an isolated breakthrough but the crowning practical conclusions of a comprehensive renovation of the marxist world view. Nor did it come a moment too soon, it now faced the crucial test of practice with the outbreak of the Russian Revolution in February 1917. The question we must ask is how did it measure up to this test?

5. The party in the revolution

The momentous events of the Russian Revolution confirmed Lenin's theory of the party in two fundamental ways. Firstly, it showed that an originally tiny organisation could, in the heat of the struggle, grow extremely rapidly and, even more important, gain the support of the overwhelming majority of the working class. In January 1917 the Bolshevik party membership stood at 23,600. By the end of April it had grown to 79,204, and in August it was estimated to be about 200,000.[75] Presumably by October it was even larger. Measured against the Russian population as a whole, 200,000 remained an almost insignificant figure, but the Bolshevik membership was concentrated in the small, but politically decisive, working class. Leonard Schapiro has recorded that: 'A sample of replies from the organisations in twenty-five towns shows that the percentage of organised Bolsheviks among the factory workers in the towns at this date (August 1917) varied from 1 per cent to 12 per cent—the average for the twenty-five towns being 5.4 per cent.'[76] For a disciplined activist party this was a very high proportion. It meant that in the key industrial centres, especially Petrograd, the Bolsheviks had complete political leadership of the proletariat. Thus the first representative body to yield a Bolshevik majority was a conference of Petrograd factory delegates at the end of May, and when the Menshevik/ SR dominated executive of the soviets called a mass demonstration in Petrograd on 18 June, about 400,000 marched and 90 per cent of the banners bore Bolshevik slogans. As for October, Lenin's old opponent Martov wrote 'Understand, please, what we have before us after all is a victorious uprising of the proletariat—almost the entire proletariat supports Lenin and expects its social liberation from the uprising.'[77] In nine months the Bolsheviks rose from a seemingly irrelevant splinter group to the most powerful political force in Russia.

Secondly, the Revolution demonstrated the indispensability of a centralised revolutionary party for the conquest of state power by the working class. The February Revolution which overthrew Tsarism and gave birth to the soviets was, of course, not led by the Bolsheviks nor by any political party. As E. H. Carr comments:

> The February Revolution . . . was the spontaneous outbreak of a multitude exasperated by the privations of the war and the manifest inequality in distribution of burdens . . . The revolutionary parties played no direct part in the making of the revolution. They did not expect it and were at first somewhat nonplussed by it. The creation at the moment of the revolution of the Petrograd Soviet of Workers' Deputies was a spontaneous act of groups of workers without central direction.[78]

But precisely because of this, the victorious revolution made by workers and soldiers (peasants in uniform), did not place power in the hands of the working class. On the contrary it voluntarily surrendered power to the bourgeoisie in the form of the Provisional Government. The workers and soldiers certainly did not like this development. 'As early as 3 March, meetings of soldiers and workers began to demand that the soviet depose forthwith the Provisional Government of the liberal bourgeoisie, and take power in its own hands'.[79] But, lacking organisation and political leadership, they were unable to impose their will. Only with the growth of the Bolsheviks into a mass party and with the emergence of a Bolshevik majority in the soviets were these embryos of workers' state power able to fulfil their potentiality. Only through a party could a clear and concise political programme—'Bread, Land, and Peace', 'All Power to the Soviets'—be formulated, capable of concretising the feelings of the masses and uniting the different strands of the revolution, the workers, the peasants and the soldiers.

Also the party was crucial for the mounting and success of the actual insurrection. In the first place, it was able through its capacity to assess the situation in Russia as a whole, its discipline and its moral authority with the workers, to prevent a premature rising in 'the July Days' which would have isolated the impetuous workers and soldiers of Petrograd from the rest of the country. Had the Bolsheviks been less disciplined and less well established they might easily have been caught up by events and dragged into a hopeless uprising which would have met the fate of the Paris Commune or the German revolution of 1919.[80] Then when, after the defeat of the Kornilov plot, the mood of the country, not just of Petrograd, had shifted in their favour, and it became clear that the Bolsheviks would have a majority at the second congress of soviets, the party was able to seize the critical moment when power could be gained swiftly and smoothly. Carr writes that, 'For the organisation of the almost bloodless victory of 25 October–7 November 1917 the Petrograd Soviet and its military-revolutionary committee were responsible.'[81] But the soviet had a Bolshevik majority and the military-revolutionary committee contained only one non-Bolshevik (a young left-SR). Moreover the initial decision to launch the insurrection, which they were implementing, was taken not by the soviet but by the central committee of the party in secret session.[82] Nor could it have been otherwise, for timing and secrecy were of the essence. A public debate in the soviet would have alerted the Provisional Government and given it the chance to take pre-emptive action. By their nature the soviets were politically heterogenous. Only a disciplined and politically united body, the party, could discuss the tactical pros and cons of the insurrection and plan its execution. And immediately after the seizure of power only the Bolshevik party possessed the unity of will and purpose to form a government capable of dealing with the immensely difficult and chaotic situation facing the revolution.

The pre-eminent role of the Bolshevik party in the October insurrection combined with the relatively small number of participants in the fighting, and the brevity of the operation (at least in the capital) have led many commentators to depict the revolution as essentially a coup d'état by a tiny but determined minority, acting quite independently of the class they claimed to represent.[83] This view seems strengthened by Lenin's repeated insistence that it was 'necessary to fight against constitutional illusions and hopes placed in the congress of soviets, to discard the preconceived idea that we absolutely must "wait" for it.'[84] Did not the actual course of the insurrection completely violate the distinction between party and state, which we discussed earlier, and did not this mean that in practice the Leninist conception of the party as a minority vanguard necessarily led to the seizure of power by that minority? In answering these questions it is necessary to look not just at the period when the whole fate of the revolution depended on a few days fighting, but at the evolution of Lenin's policy throughout 1917. Lenin first set the Bolsheviks on course for the conquest of power with his 'April Theses', but from the start he guarded himself 'against any kind of Blanquist adventurism'.[85] 'In the theses', wrote Lenin, 'I very definitely reduced the question to one of a struggle for influence within the Soviets of Workers', Agricultural Labourers', Peasants' and Soldiers' Deputies. To leave no shadow of doubt on this score, I twice emphasised in the theses the need for patient and persistent "explanatory" work "adapted to the practical needs of the masses".'[86] 'Patient explanation' remained the line of Lenin and the Bolsheviks through the spring and summer of 1917, and always the struggle for power was linked to winning over the soviets. Even when in July Lenin considered that the soviets had moved decisively into the anti-revolutionary camp and therefore wanted to withdraw the slogan 'All Power to the Soviets', he was still careful to warn that 'a decisive struggle will be possible only in the event of a new revolutionary upsurge in the very depths of the masses'.[87] Nor did he then abandon the soviet idea. 'Soviets may appear in this new revolution, and indeed are bound to, but *not* the present soviets, not organs collaborating with the bourgeoisie, but organs of revolutionary struggle against the bourgeoisie. It is true that even then we shall be in favour of building the whole state on the model of the soviets.'[88] Only when the Bolsheviks had achieved a majority in the soviets did Lenin place insurrection on the order of the day.

The fact that it was primarily the party, acting through the Petrograd Soviet, that effected the rising did not contradict this perspective because this was essentially a destructive operation. The new structure of state power was already in existence and recognised as the supreme authority by both the workers and the army. The action on the night of 24/25 October merely eliminated the Provisional Government, leaving the soviets as the sole power. Furthermore, it was on their soviet majority, not the right of armed conquest, that the Bolsheviks based their claim to form the government. On 5 November Lenin wrote:

> There must be no other government in Russia but a soviet government. Soviet power has been won in Russia and the government can be transferred out of the hands of one soviet party into the hands of another party without any revolution, simply by a decision of the soviets, simply by new elections of deputies to the soviets. The Bolshevik party was in the majority at the Second All-Russian Congress of Soviets. Only a government formed by that party is, therefore, a soviet government.[89]

Thus, in general, the practical test of the Russian Revolution brilliantly confirmed Lenin's theory of the party. It completely justified his conviction that a principled and disciplined vanguard would play a decisive role in the achievement of the socialist revolution. But here a note of caution must be sounded, for the process by which the Bolshevik party actually came to play this role was not at all automatic.

Before Lenin's return to Russia, the Bolshevik leadership slipped into a position of conditional support for the Provisional Government and also for the war. When Lenin first declared in favour of the overthrow of the Provisional Government and 'All Power to the Soviets', he found no support from within the party's leading circles. The latter, basing themselves on the longstanding Bolshevik formula of 'the democratic dictatorship of the proletariat and the peasantry', denounced Lenin's position as 'unacceptable' in *Pravda*. Even the most meticulously prepared revolutionary party could not anticipate all the concrete features of the revolution, and therefore had to learn from reality and from the workers. Within the party leadership Lenin was the agent of this learning process. 'Theory my friend, is grey, but green is the eternal tree of life',[90] wrote Lenin, condemning 'those "old Bolsheviks" who more than once already have played so regrettable a role in the history of our party by reiterating formulas senselessly learned by rote, instead of studying the specific features of the new and living reality'.[91] That, starting from a position of seeming isolation, Lenin so rapidly won over the party to his position was due partly to his great personal prestige, but also to the fact that he was articulating theoretically the views of the advanced workers who were flooding into the party. Lenin's tirades against the 'old Bolsheviks' dovetailed with the pressure coming up from the factory districts. Repeatedly through 1917 Lenin would comment that the party was to the left of its central committee, and the masses were to the left of the party.

Even after Lenin had won the victory in principle at the April Conference, sections of the party continued to vacillate, and this was most marked in relation to the question of insurrection. Kamenev, Zinoviev, Nogin, Miliutin and Ryhov formed a group within the leadership completely opposed to the staging of an insurrection.[92] Kamenev and Zinoviev stood, next to Lenin, as the party's most authoritative leaders, and yet at the decisive moment they wavered. It took a month of battering by Lenin, including threats that he would resign and campaign among the rank-and-file,[93] to overcome this opposition and shake the central committee out of its inertia. When, immediately after the seizure of power, the Zinoviev-Kamenev group demanded that the Bolsheviks enter a coalition with the Mensheviks and SRs, Lenin once again threatened a split ('an honest and open split would now be incomparably better than internal sabotage, the thwarting of our own decisions, disorganisation and prostration'[94]) and declared that if the opposition had a majority in the party, they should form their coalition government and he would 'go to the sailors'.

That sections of the Bolshevik party and at times the party as a whole, faltered in this way, does not, of course, invalidate the principles on which it had been built. Neither before nor since has any working-class party acquitted itself better in the conditions of revolutionary upheaval. But it does mean that the organisation of the party on Leninist lines is not, in itself, any guarantee of success. It is not an organisational key which opens all the doors of history. The revolutionary party is indispensable, but the most revolutionary of parties is subject to an element of conservative routinism simply because it has to be a permanent stable organisation. Equally the very creation of a party as a distinct body involves the risk that the party may separate itself from the class. The advantage of the Leninist party was that though it could not exclude these dangers it reduced them to a minimum. The greatness of Lenin in the Russian Revolution was that he—the party man par excellence— in the last analysis transcended his party. He was able, so to speak, to reach over the head of the party to the mass of the Russian workers and soldiers, not so much to address them as to respond to them, and so was able to force the party to respond as well. Expressing this idea as a theoretical generalisation one can say that for Lenin, although the party had often to maintain a high degree of autonomy vis-à-vis the working class, and although the claims of the party and its discipline were strong, in the final analysis the party remained subordinate to, and dependent upon, the class. The Leninist theory of the party in no way implies the fetishisation of party loyalty that characterised social democracy and was later to assume the most grotesque forms and dimensions in the official Communist Parties of the Soviet Union and the world.

6. The single world party

Lenin's theory of the party was, we have argued, in its essentials fully formed by the beginning of 1917. Now with the theory vindicated by the October Revolution Lenin possessed the political authority and influence to bring into being the logical conclusion of that theory, namely the Communist International. The first congress of the Communist International opened in Moscow on the 2 March 1919, but in reality this was little more than the planting of a banner and a declaration of intent. Only 35 delegates attended and most of these were from the small nations that formerly were part of the Russian empire. Not until the second congress in July 1920, which 217 delegates attended, did the new International take definite shape as a mass fighting organisation. The leadership of the Communist International was, naturally, the work of many hands and Lenin frequently took a back seat. Zinoviev was its president and many of its most important manifestoes were written by

Trotsky. Nonetheless it is quite legitimate to consider the work of the Communist International in a study of Lenin's theory of the party, as he was both its initiator and most ardent champion (sometimes even against his own supporters) and certainly either inspired or approved all its most important strategic decisions.[95] The discussion here will be extremely brief and inadequate. There are two reasons for this: firstly, an adequate treatment of all the questions of party strategy, tactics and organisation dealt with by the International in its first few years would require at least a book to itself; secondly, we have been concerned primarily with the *development* of Lenin's theory of the party, and the work of the International involved in the main the *application* of ideas we have already discussed. Consequently only the main outlines will be indicated here, with the emphasis on those aspects of the Comintern which were in some way new departures.

The most immediately striking difference between the Second and Third Internationals, as organisations, lay in the fact that the former was a loose federation of independent national parties, whereas the latter was to be strictly centralised. As the Statutes adopted at the second congress put it: 'The Communist International must, in fact and in deed, be a single communist party of the entire world. The parties working in the various countries are but its separate sections.'[96] Supreme authority was vested in the world congress to meet regularly once a year, but in between congresses the International was to be run by its elected Executive Committee, which was given extensive powers.

> The Executive Committee conducts the entire work of the Communist International from one congress to the next...and issues instructions which are binding on all parties and organisations belonging to the Communist International. The Executive Committee of the Communist International shall expel groups or persons who offend against international discipline, and it also has the right to expel from the Communist International those parties which violate decisions of the world congress.[97]

This conception of the International as a centralised world party was a major advance. In part it was designed to prevent any repetition of the nationalist fragmentation that destroyed the Second International in 1914. More positively its aim was to create a unified general staff of what was assumed to be the impending world revolution. Trotsky has neatly summarised the thinking that lay behind this form of organisation.

Lenin's internationalism is not a formula for harmonising national and international interests in empty verbiage. It is a guide to revolutionary action embracing all nations. Our planet, inhabited by so-called civilised humanity, is considered as one single battlefield where various nations and social classes contend.[98]

One battlefield required one army and one high command. The Communist International was to be, as Lukacs has put it, 'The Bolshevik Party—Lenin's concept of the party—on a world scale.'[99]

To realise this aim it was necessary to foster the rapid growth of genuine revolutionary parties in all the main capitalist countries. To do this the Comintern worked to draw together existing Communist groups and trends and unite them into stable parties, and to win over as large a proportion as possible of the rank-and-file of Europe's socialist parties (notably the USPD, the Italian Socialist Party (PSI) and the French Socialist Party). In this process the main enemy was 'centrism',[100] in that the centrist leaders had to be discredited to capture their supporters, and in that they had to be prevented from entering the International and infecting it. It was precisely the pressure from the rank-and-file in favour of the International that drew reformists in its direction and created this latter danger. At the second congress Lenin warned that 'The Communist International is, to a certain extent, becoming the vogue . . . [and] may be faced with the danger of dilution by the influx of wavering and irresolute groups that have not as yet broken with their Second International ideology.'[101] Just as in 1903 Lenin had insisted on Clause 1 of the Party Rules as a weapon against opportunism, he now drew up 21 conditions of admission to the Communist International. These were extremely stringent. Condition 2 demanded that 'Any organisation that wishes to join the Communist International must consistently and systematically dismiss reformists and "centrists" from positions of any responsibility in the working-class movement.'[102] Condition 4 insisted on 'systematic propaganda and agitation . . . in the armed forces'.[103] Condition 14 required that 'Communist parties in countries where communists can conduct their work legally must carry out periodic membership purges (re-registrations) with the aim of systematically ridding the party of petty-bourgeois elements that inevitably percolate into them.' Summing up the 21 conditions, Zinoviev declared, 'Just as it is not easy for a camel to pass through the eye of a needle, so, I hope, it will not be easy for the adherents of the centre to slip through the 21 conditions.'[104] Prominent leaders of the centre, Crispien and Dittmann from the USPD and Serrati from the PSI, were present at the congress but their objections were forcefully rebutted by Lenin as 'fundamentally Kautskyan . . . [and] imbued with a bourgeois spirit'.[105]

Parallel to the struggle against centrism, there was a debate with various revolutionary but ultra-left or syndicalist tendencies. This was conducted in a much more friendly fashion. The errors of the 'Left' were put down primarily to their 'youth' and inexperience. Some of the 'Left', notably Pestaña from the Spanish syndicalists and Tanner from the British Shop Stewards' Movement, were so disgusted by the opportunism of the social-democratic parties that they rejected altogether the need for a proletarian party. In reply Lenin, Trotsky and Zinoviev patiently set out the ABC of the Leninist theory of the party, stressing the contrast between a social-democratic and a communist party.[106] It is noticeable that there were no tirades against 'economism' and no mention of the 'introduction of socialism into the working class from without'. The adopted theses stated 'The revolutionary syndicalists often speak of the great part that can be played by a determined revolutionary minority. A really determined minority of the working class, a minority that is communist, that wants to act, that has a programme, that is out to organise the struggle of the masses—that is precisely what the communist party is.'[107]

More difficult and more instructive was the argument with those who accepted the need for a revolutionary party but who wanted it to pursue a simon-pure policy of no compromise, no manoeuvres and no participation in bourgeois parliaments or reactionary trade unions— this was the line of the KAPD (recently split from the German CP), Bordiga in Italy, Gorter and Pannekoek in Holland, Gallacher and Sylvia Pankhurst in Britain. To Lenin all this was 'old and familiar rubbish',[108] but his reply, *Left Wing Communism—An Infantile Disorder*, specially written for the second congress, was one of his most thorough and lucid expositions of the strategy and tactics of the revolutionary party. Recounting some of the lesser-known episodes in the history of Bolshevism, Lenin argued that it was necessary to remain in the trade unions and 'carry on communist work within them at all costs',[109] and that 'whilst you lack the strength to do away with bourgeois parliaments and every other type of reactionary institution you *must* work within them'.[110] 'The task devolving on Communists', he wrote, 'is to *convince* the backward elements, to work among them, and not to fence themselves off from them with artificial and childishly "Left" slogans.'[111] Lenin was concerned that communists should not 'regard what is obsolete to us as something obsolete to a class, to the masses'.[112]

The concept of the party presented by Lenin in *Left Wing Communism* is that not of a band of blinkered dogmatists marching in only one direction—straight forward—but of a highly aware and politically astute body able to manoeuvre, at times to compromise and to retreat, so as never to lose contact with the class it aims to lead, and yet able 'through all the intermediate stations and all compromises . . . [to] clearly perceive and constantly pursue the final aim'.[113] Of course it would not always be easy to distinguish between compromises that were necessary and those that were treacherous, but 'It would be absurd to formulate a recipe or general rule ("No compromises") to suit all cases'.[114] What was required, Lenin argued, was analysis of the concrete situation.

> It is, in fact, one of the functions of a party organisation and of party leaders worthy of the name, to acquire, through the prolonged, persistent, variegated and comprehensive efforts of all thinking representatives of a given class, the knowledge, experience and—in addition to knowledge and experience—the political flair necessary for the speedy and correct solution of complex political problems.[115]

During 1919 and 1920 the main emphasis within the Comintern was placed on the struggle against opportunism with ultra-leftism being regarded as a much less serious deviation, but in 1921 this changed. Throughout Europe the working-class movement had been split and the opportunists and centrists had been expelled from the International— now the emphasis shifted to combating 'leftism'. The basic reason for this was the change in the objective situation. The immediate post-war period had seen an international wave of direct revolutionary struggles and the bourgeoisie had been thrown into panic. The perspective of the International was one of immediate world revolution. But in country after country the working class had been beaten back and the bourgeoisie had regained confidence. In all cases the new communist parties had conspicuously failed to win the support of the majority of the working class.

The immediate catalyst of the reorientation of Comintern strategy was the disastrous March action of the KPD in 1921. Over-reacting to the deliberately provocative police occupation of the Mansfield coal mines, the German Communist leaders attempted, without preparation and without majority support, to call a general strike and transform it into an uprising. When the workers failed to respond, party members were ordered to force them on to the streets and the unemployed, amongst whom the party had a strong base, were used to occupy factories against the will of the workers. The result was heavy fighting between communist and non-communist workers, the complete rout of the former and the decimation of the party (membership fell by almost two-thirds).[116] Not content with this the KPD's 'left' leadership attempted to generalise their ludicrous adventurism into a system going under the name 'the theory of the offensive'.

Clearly it was time to call a halt. Lenin declared that if the 'theorists of the offensive' constituted a definite trend, then 'a relentless fight against this trend is essential, for otherwise there is no Communist International'.[117] The third congress of the International in June–July 1921 adopted the slogan 'To the masses' and stated that 'The most important question before the Communist International today is to win predominating influence over the majority of the working class.'[118] Particular attention was now to be paid to 'partial struggles and partial demands'. 'The task of the communist parties is to extend, to deepen, and to unify this struggle for concrete demands . . . These partial demands, anchored in the needs of the broadest masses, must be put forward by the communist parties in a way which not only leads the masses to struggle, but by its very nature organises them.'[119] The logical consequence of this new line was the policy of the united front, which was promulgated by the Executive of the International in December 1921 and ratified by the fourth congress in 1922. The idea of the united front was that public approaches should be made to the leaders of the social-democratic parties proposing united action on a common programme of basic economic and political demands arising from the immediate needs of the working class. If the social democrats agreed, then the communist parties would have the chance to prove in practice their superiority as defenders of the proletariat. If the social democrats rejected the proposals, then the blame for any disunity would fall on them. But as well as being an indirect weapon against the social democrats, the united front was also designed to reconcile the existence of separate communist parties with the need of the working class for unity in the day-to-day struggle against the industrialists and the state.[120]

In order that the parties of the International should be able more effectively to carry out this day-to-day agitation for immediate demands and to lend it a revolutionary character, and to be better prepared for future revolutionary opportunities, it was thought necessary that they should 'bolshevise' not only their ideology, strategy and tactics, but also the details of their organisation and methods of work. We discussed earlier the differences between the organisation of the pre-revolutionary Bolshevik party and that current in the European social-democratic parties. In 1921 many of the Western CPs were still functioning on the social-democratic model. To correct this the third congress adopted theses on 'The Organisation and Construction of Communist Parties' which were to be implemented by each national section. Apart from general remarks about democratic centralism the theses stressed the obligation of all members to work, the key role of factory and trade-union cells, the importance of report backs on all activity and the necessity of an illegal communications network, and gave instructions on how to prepare for meetings and work in trade-union branches.

Organising millions of workers in a single world party, the Communist International, during its first few years marks in many respects the highest point that has yet been achieved by the marxist revolutionary movement. And yet it was also a failure; not just in that it did not produce immediate world revolution, but also in that within a few years it ceased to be a revolutionary force at all and became the submissive instrument of Russian foreign policy. Russian domination was the rock on which the Communist International foundered. It was of course inevitable that the leaders of the world's first successful workers' revolution would be listened to with respect. Moreover this was, at first, a positive factor as the Russian leaders, especially Lenin and Trotsky, were clearly superior in theory and in practical experience to anyone in the new European parties. Lenin frankly acknowledged the fact of Russian leadership, but assumed that it would be only temporary. 'Leadership in the revolutionary proletarian International has passed for a time—for a short time, it goes without saying—to the Russians, just as at various periods of the nineteenth century it was in the hands of the British, then of the French, then of the Germans.'[121] As long as the Russian Revolution linked its fate to the success of the revolution internationally,[122] the pre-eminence of the

Russian leaders aided the International, but as soon as this orientation was abandoned the International was ruined.

Two factors explain the continued passive submission of the foreign communist parties to Russian direction. The first was the series of defeats inflicted on the international working-class movement. The Russians alone retained the prestige of success, and on the basis of nothing but setbacks no other party developed the confidence or authority to challenge them. The second was a failure of the Bolsheviks to communicate, or, put the other way round, a failure of the foreign parties to learn. The communists of Germany, Italy, France, etc. found themselves continually being criticised and corrected, first from the left and then from the right. In the process they seem to have absorbed not the Leninist method as a whole, on which the corrections were based, but only the idea that Moscow was always right. Consequently they never developed the capacity for independent concrete analysis which Lenin considered to be a function of the party to produce in its leaders. In his last speech to the Communist International in November 1922, Lenin seemed to be beginning to grapple with this problem, though he did not have the chance to develop his ideas.

> At the third congress in 1921, we adopted a resolution on the organisational structure of the communist parties and on the methods and content of their activities. The resolution is an excellent one, but is almost entirely Russian, that is to say, everything in it is based on Russian conditions. This is its good point but it is also its failing. It is its failing because I am sure that no foreigner can read it . . . and . . . if by way of exception some foreigner does understand it, he cannot carry it out . . . we have not learnt how to present our Russian experience to foreigners . . . the most important thing for all of us, Russian and foreign comrades alike, is to sit down and study . . . We are studying in the general sense. They, however, must study in the special sense, in order that they may really understand the organisational structure, method and content of revolutionary work.[123]

The failure of the International and its transformation into the tool of the emergent Russian state bureaucracy, does not discredit the concept of the centralised world party, for that concept was the reflection of the international nature of the class struggle. But it does show that the creation of an International intensifies not only the advantages, but also the dangers inherent in the creation of a party at all. A healthy International would have been a powerful counterweight to the processes of degeneration at work in Russia. As it was, the International proved a reliable prop and support for the Stalinist bureaucracy. What remained from the early years of the Communist International was, in Trotsky's words, 'an invaluable programmatic heritage'.[124] To this one can add that its documents, its theses, its debates and in some respects its practice give us the most complete picture of the application of the fully developed Leninist theory of the party.

7. The essence of Lenin's theory

From the foregoing account it is clear that Lenin's theory of the party was a highly complex, many-faceted doctrine. We have argued that to understand this theory fully it is necessary to trace its evolution relating each step in its development to the practical and theoretical problems which engendered it. This we have attempted to do and on this basis it is possible to venture a brief summary of the essence of the theory.

There are two basic themes in Lenin's theory of the party: first, the absolutely independent organisation of the advanced workers, rigidly upholding the overall interests of the working class and all the exploited and the ultimate aim of international socialist revolution; second, the closest possible relationship with the mass of workers maintained by providing practical leadership in every struggle involving the workers or affecting their interests. The former means fixed adherence to principle, a willingness to accept, for a period, the position of a tiny and apparently isolated minority, and the waging of an unrelenting struggle within the working class against all manifestations of opportunism. The latter means extreme tactical flexibility and the ability to exploit every avenue to maintain contact with the masses.

These two elements are not separate but dialectically interrelated and mutually dependent. Without firm principles and disciplined organisation the party will either be unable to execute the necessary abrupt tactical turns or will be derailed by them. Without deep involvement in the struggles of the working class the party will be unable to forge and maintain its discipline and will become subject to the pressure of alien classes. Unless the day-to-day struggle of the working class is linked to the ultimate aim of the overthrow of capitalism, it will fail in its purpose. Unless the party can relate the ultimate aim to immediate struggles, it will degenerate into a useless sect. The more developed the spontaneous activity of the workers, the more it demands conscious revolutionary organisation on pain of catastrophic defeat. But revolutionary organisation cannot be maintained and renewed unless it receives the infusion of fresh blood from the spontaneous revolt of the masses.

All the organisational forms characteristic of Bolshevism—the close watch on the party's boundaries, the commitment to activity of all members, the strict discipline, the full inner-party democracy, the primary role of the workplace cell, the combination of legal and illegal work—derive from the need to combine these two elements. The Leninist party is the concrete expression of the marxist synthesis of determinism and voluntarism in revolutionary practice.

Throughout Lenin's revolutionary career the two aspects outlined here were continually present, but at different times one aspect preponderated over the other in his concerns. In 1903 and 1914 and at the first two congresses of the Communist International it was the independence of the party that was dominant. In 1905 and at the third and fourth congresses of the International it was the relationship with the masses. In October 1917 the two were inextricably fused precisely because the revolution marked the fusion in the working class of its immediate demands and its historical interests. Part of Lenin's unique genius was his ability to judge which aspect to stress, which way to 'bend the stick' at a particular time.

'It is not enough' he wrote, 'to be a revolutionary and an advocate of socialism in general. It is necessary to know at every moment how to find the particular link in the chain which must be grasped with all one's strength in order to keep the whole chain in place and prepare to move on resolutely to the next link.'[125]

Of all marxists Lenin unquestionably made the largest and most significant contribution to the development of the theory of the party. His ideas transformed the organisation, strategy and tactics of first the Russian and then the world working-class movement. They are the criteria by which, and to a large extent the framework within which, all other contributions to the theory of the party, including that of Marx, must be assessed.

4.
Rosa Luxemburg's alternative view

Lenin's theory of the party has had many critics and opponents both from outside and from within the working-class movement, but its most important critic and the most articulate proponent of an alternative view of the party, *who was also a revolutionary socialist*, was Rosa Luxemburg.

1. Polemics against Lenin—the spontaneity of the masses

Rosa Luxemburg was a Polish revolutionary who spent the most important years of her life as theoretical leader of the extreme left of German Social Democracy. In 1899 she emerged, with her pamphlet *Social Reform or Revolution*, as the principal opponent of Bernsteinian revisionism, and thereafter she increasingly recognised and fought against the inertia and conservatism of the Kautskyite centre. But it was her close interest in the development of the Russian socialist movement[1] that led her to formulate her own distinctive view of the role of the revolutionary party and its relationship to the working class. Disturbed by the 1903 split in the Russian party and by what she regarded as Lenin's 'ultra-centralism', she took issue with Lenin in a famous pamphlet, written in 1904, called *Organisational Questions of Russian Social Democracy*.[2]

In this work she begins, as a marxist should, by situating the problem of party organisation firmly in the context of the peculiar tasks and problems facing the proletarian movement as a whole in Russia. Because, she argues, Russia has not yet achieved a bourgeois revolution and still suffers the domination of an absolute monarchy, the proletariat has not had the benefit of the political education and organisation that a period of bourgeois democracy inevitably brings. In Russia, therefore, she writes:

The social democracy must make up by its own efforts an entire historical period. It must lead the Russian proletarians from their present 'atomised' condition, which prolongs the autocratic regime, to a class organisation that would help them to become aware of their historic objectives and prepare them to struggle to achieve those objectives . . . Like God Almighty they must have this organisation arise out of the void, so to speak.[3]

In this context of a struggle against the disconnected clubs and local groups characteristic of the past period in Russia, she finds it 'understandable why the slogan of persons who want to see an inclusive national organisation should be "centralism".'[4]

But, she warns, 'Centralism does not completely cover the question of organisation for Russian Social Democracy.'[5] For although, 'it is undeniable that a strong tendency towards centralisation is inherent in the social-democratic movement (springing from the economic make up of capitalism)'[6], it can be carried to a point when it hinders the unfettered development and initiative of the working class itself.

The social-democratic movement is the first in the history of class societies which reckons, in all its phases and through its entire course, on the organisation and the direct, independent action of the masses. Because of this, social democracy creates an organisational type that is entirely different from those common to earlier revolutionary movements, such as those of the Jacobins and the adherents of Blanqui.[7]

Because the proletariat learns and develops both its class-consciousness and its organisation in the course of the struggle itself,

there do not exist detailed sets of tactics which a Central Committee can teach the party membership in the same way as troops are instructed in their training camps.[8]

For this reason social-democratic centralism cannot be based on the mechanical subordination and blind obedience of the party membership to the leading party centre. For this reason the social-democratic movement cannot allow the erection of an air-tight partition between the class-conscious nucleus of the proletariat already in the party and its immediate popular environment, the non-party sections of the proletariat.[9]

Lenin, Rosa Luxemburg argues, has forgotten or does not appreciate this basic distinction between the organisation of social democracy and that of Jacobinism or Blanquism. In opposition to Lenin's dictum that the revolutionary social democrat is nothing other than a 'Jacobin indissolubly joined to the organisation of the proletariat, which has become conscious of its class interests', she writes 'The fact is that the social democracy is not *joined* to the organisation of the proletariat. It is itself the proletariat.'[10] Therefore at all costs it must not be straitjacketed by an ultra-centralised and disciplined form of organisation, but allowed free rein to develop. The great forward steps of the movement in terms of tactics and methods of struggle are not invented by leaders or by a central committee, but are the 'spontaneous product of the movement in ferment'.[11]

> The unconscious comes before the conscious. The logic of the historic process comes before the subjective logic of the human beings who participate in the historic process. The tendency is for the directing organs of the socialist party to play a conservative role.[12]

For Luxemburg, Lenin's failure to appreciate this conservative tendency was particularly dangerous in Russian conditions where the proletarian movement was young and as yet not fully matured in its political education.

> To attempt to bind the initiative of the party at this moment, to surround it with a network of barbed wire, is to render it incapable of accomplishing the tremendous tasks of the hour . . . [13]
>
> Nothing will more surely enslave a young labour movement to an intellectual elite hungry for power than this bureaucratic strait-jacket, which will immobilise the movement and turn it into an automaton manipulated by a Central Committee.[14]

In addition to these general warnings on the dangers of Lenin's 'ultra-centralism', Luxemburg also takes up the question of the party rules and opportunism. Echoing the arguments of Trotsky (see Chapter 2 above), she dismisses 'the idea that the road to opportunism can be barred by means of clauses in a party constitution'.[15] Opportunism is an historic product and an inevitable phase of the movement. She maintains that: 'It is naïve to hope to stop this current by means of a formula written down in a constitution.'[16]

Concluding her critique of Lenin's organisational theses, Luxemburg returns to her starting point, situating the dispute in the overall development of the class struggle in Russia in an eloquent and memorable passage.

> In Lenin's overanxious desire to establish the guardianship of an omniscient omnipotent Central Committee in order to protect so promising and vigorous a labour movement from any mis-step, we recognise symptoms of the same subjectivism that has already played more than one trick on socialist thinking in Russia.
>
> It is amusing to note the strange somersaults that the respectable human 'ego' has had to perform in recent Russian history. Knocked to the ground, almost reduced to dust by Russian absolutism, the 'ego' takes revenge by turning to revolutionary activity. In the shape of a committee of conspirators, in the name of a non-existent Will of the People, it seats itself on a kind of throne and proclaims it is all-powerful. But the 'object' proves to be the stronger. The knout is triumphant, for czarist might seems to be 'legitimate' expression of history.
>
> In time we see appear on the scene an even more 'legitimate' child of history—the Russian labour movement. For the first time bases for the formation of a real 'people's will' are laid in Russian soil.
>
> But here is the 'ego' of the Russian revolutionary again! Pirouetting on its head, it once more proclaims itself to be the all-powerful director of history—this time with the title of His Excellency the Central Committee of the Social Democratic Party of Russia.
>
> The nimble acrobat fails to perceive that the only 'subject' which merits today the role of director is the collective 'ego' of the working class. The working class demands the right to make mistakes and learn in the dialectic of history.
>
> Let us speak plainly. Historically, the errors committed by a truly revolutionary movement are infinitely more fruitful than the infallibility of the cleverest Central Committee.[17]

Thus, for Luxemburg, Lenin's whole organisational plan was a subjectivist or voluntarist (in philosophical terms, idealist) deviation from an historical materialist approach produced by the combination of an immature proletarian movement and the enormous tasks facing it. Against Lenin's emphasis on the role of the party and its leadership, she stressed the potentially conservative role of such a body and contrasted it to the revolutionary spontaneity of the masses in struggle.

Rosa Luxemburg developed these themes further in her pamphlet, *The Mass Strike, the Political Party and the Trade Unions*, written in 1906, to explain to the German working class the significance of the events of the previous year in Russia. It shows how many of the ideas posed theoretically and generally in *Organisational Questions of Russian Social Democracy* became concrete reality in the enormous revolutionary upheaval that was Russia in 1905. Above all it is a celebration of the initiative and daring with which the working class finds solutions to problems that have baffled the theorists for decades.

1905, Luxemburg showed, was merely the culmination of five years of turmoil in which Russia was continually aflame with mass strikes. These strikes were the outward manifestation of the inner maturation of the revolution itself. Often they began without any preparation or even strike funds and, contrary to all previous schemes, rather than following upon trade-union organisation, they preceded it and gave it a powerful impetus. Often, also, the immediate cause was a minor grievance; the mass strike of January 1905 in St Petersburg which led to the march on the Winter Palace began over the sacking of two men at the Putilov Works. What united all these actions was their spontaneity. They had no predetermined plan and were not called for by any party or body of leaders and were only possible because the revolution itself had unleashed hitherto undreamed of initiative, courage and self-sacrifice in the masses. An attempt, Luxemburg noted, at the end of the movement, by the Central Committee of the RSDLP, to call a mass strike over the opening of the Duma, fell absolutely flat.

Also central to Luxemburg's critique of established preconceptions of the class struggle was her attack on the mechanical separation of the economic and political struggles (a dichotomy clearly present in *What is to be done?*). The Russian workers had not conformed to these categories either.

> But the movement as a whole does not proceed from the economic to the political struggle, nor even the reverse. Every great political mass action, after it has attained its political highest point, breaks up into a mass of economic strikes. And that applies not only to each of the great mass strikes, but also to the revolution as a whole. With the spreading, clarifying and involution of the political struggle, the economic struggle not only does not recede, but extends, organises and becomes involved in equal measure. Between the two there is the most complete reciprocal action . . .
>
> Every new onset and every fresh victory of the political struggle is transformed into a powerful impetus for the economic struggle . . . And

conversely. The workers' condition of ceaseless economic struggle with the capitalists keeps their fighting energy alive in every political interval . . .

In a word, the economic struggle is the transmitter from one political centre to another; the political struggle is the periodic fertilisation of the soil for the economic struggle. Cause and effect here continually change places; and thus the economic and the political factor in the period of the mass strike now widely removed, completely separated or even mutually exclusive, as the theoretical plan would have them, merely form the two interlacing sides of the proletarian class struggle in Russia.[18]

As we can see, *The Mass Strike* pamphlet is of a piece with the polemic against Lenin. Just as Lenin's organisational plan was subjectivist, so are those who seek to plan mass strikes. Her main theme in both works is to warn against overestimating the capacities of the party and especially the party leadership.

There are quite definite limits set to initiative and conscious direction. During the revolution it is extremely difficult for any directing organ of the proletarian movement to foresee and to calculate which occasions and factors can lead to explosions and which cannot. Here also initiative and direction do not consist in issuing commands according to one's inclinations, but in the most adroit adaptability to the given situation, and the closest possible contact with the mood of the masses.[19]

Twelve years later Rosa Luxemburg returned to essentially the same ideas when, in her work *The Russian Revolution*, she criticised the Bolsheviks for their restrictions on democracy.

The tacit assumption underlying the Lenin-Trotsky theory of the dictatorship is this: that the socialist transformation is something for which a ready-made formula lies completed in the pocket of the revolutionary party, which needs only to be carried out energetically in practice. This is unfortunately—or perhaps fortunately—not the case . . . The socialist system of society should only be, and can only be, a historical product, born out of the school of its own experiences, born in the course of its realisation, as a result of the developments of living history . . . The whole mass of the people must take part in it. Otherwise, socialism will be decreed from behind a few official desks by a dozen intellectuals.[20]

2. The role of the party

From this passionate emphasis on the self-activity and initiative of the working class, which dominated all her political thought and action, what conclusions did Rosa Luxemburg draw as to the role and nature of the revolutionary party? To answer this question it is first of all necessary to be clear as to the conclusions she did *not* draw, for she has so often been misrepresented on this score by would-be supporters and critics alike.

She did not, as has frequently been suggested, propound a theory of purely spontaneous revolution in which the revolutionary party and political leadership were irrelevant. This is easy to establish for her whole political career and practically everything she wrote testifies against it. From when, as little more than a schoolgirl, she joined the Polish Proletariat Party to the end of her life, she was *always* a member of a political party. Indeed the SDKPL, organised by her closest comrade Leo Jogiches in conditions similar to those in Russia, was extremely hard, centralised and conspiratorial. In *Organisational Questions of Russian Social Democracy* she wrote that 'social democracy is, as a rule, hostile to any manifestations of localism or federalism. It strives to unite all workers and all worker organisations in a single party.'[21]

In *The Mass Strike* she devoted a section of the pamphlet to arguing the need for united action between the trade unions and the Social Democratic Party under the general authority of the party.[22] After 1914 and the collapse of the Second International into chauvinism, Luxemburg, like Lenin, advocated the building of a *centralised* as against a federal International. At the end of *The Junius Pamphlet* she wrote in the appended *Theses on the Tasks of International Social Democracy*.

> 3. The centre of gravity of the organisation of the proletariat as a class is the International. The International decides in time of peace the tactics to be adopted by national sections on the questions of militarism, colonial policy, commercial policy, and the celebration of May Day, and finally, the collective tactic to be followed in the event of war.
> 4. The obligation to carry out the decisions of the International takes precedence over all else. National sections which do not conform with this place themselves outside the International.[23]

From this it is clear that Rosa Luxemburg recognised the need for the working class to be led by a revolutionary party every bit as much as did Lenin. It was in the conception of what kind of party this was to be and what its tasks were that the differences with Lenin lay. Because of her supreme confidence in the abilities of the workers in struggle, she saw the principal tasks of the party in terms of political leadership *as opposed to* the issuing of calls to action and the actual organisation of the struggle. 'Instead of puzzling their heads with the technical side, with the mechanism, of the mass strike, the social democrats are called upon to assume *political leadership* in the midst of the revolutionary period.'[24]

Essentially this is a propagandistic conception of the tasks of the party and this has implications for the degree of centralism and discipline required by the party organisation. The strict discipline demanded by Lenin was above all to achieve unity in action. A party which generally speaking restricted itself to propaganda would have no need of such a stern regime; the free play of ideas would be much more important. One of the best illustrations of the difference between Luxemburg and Lenin in this respect is the contrast in their attitudes to party administration and routine. Lenin was always intensely involved in all the minutiae of party organisation, finance and the preparation of congresses, but Luxemburg took hardly any part in these matters in either the Polish or German parties. Her biographer, Nettl, writes:

> At some stage a formal party decision (by the SDKPL) was reached that she should not concern herself with organisational matters at all, that she should not participate in any of the official conferences or congresses.[25]

Also, because her mind was focused on the task of propaganda, the distinction between the party member subject to the discipline of the party organisation and the party's supporters or sympathisers, which was so vital for Lenin, concerned her much less, as her warning against 'the erection of an air-tight partition' between the party members and their 'immediate popular environment' showed.

Thus for Luxemburg the influence of the party over the proletariat was to be exercised primarily through its ideas, its programme and its slogans rather than through the power of its organisation or its own initiation of actions, whereas in Lenin these two elements were much more evenly balanced.

It is important to keep these differences between Luxemburg and Lenin, significant though they were, in perspective. The attempt has been made to suggest that Luxemburg's divergence from Lenin over the nature of the party made her in some way fundamentally separate from the mainstream of revolutionary marxism in the twentieth century— that she represented a democratic, almost liberal, version of marxism as opposed to the dictatorial intransigence of Lenin. Bertram D. Wolfe, one of the leading proponents of this view, writes in his introduction to *The Russian Revolution and Marxism and Leninism*:

> Though they [Lenin and Luxemburg] were both called 'revolutionary' socialists, their diverse temperaments, and differing attitudes on the nature of socialist leadership, on party organisation, and on the initiative and self-activity of the working class, kept them poles apart.[26]

The argument here is that Luxemburg's objections to Lenin's 'ultra-centralism' were fundamental whereas their agreement as revolutionary socialists was something accidental or superficial. But this is a gross distortion, perpetrated so as to enlist Rosa Luxemburg in the ideological battle of the cold war. It is conclusively refuted in the very document that Wolfe advances as his main piece of evidence, *The Russian Revolution*.[27]

> The Bolsheviks have shown that they are capable of everything that a genuine revolutionary party can contribute within the limits of the historical possibilities . . . It is not a matter of this or that secondary question of tactics, but of the capacity for action of the proletariat, the strength to act, the will to power of socialism as such. In this Lenin and Trotsky and their friends were the *first*, those who went ahead as an example to the proletariat of the world; they are still the *only ones* up to now who can cry with Hutten 'I have dared'.
>
> This is essential and *enduring* in Bolshevik policy. In *this* sense theirs is the immortal historical service of having marched at the head of the international proletariat with the conquest of political power and the practical placing of the problem of the realisation of socialism, and of having advanced mightily the settling of the score between capital and labour in the entire world. In Russia the problem could only be posed. It could not be solved in Russia. And in *this* sense, the future everywhere belongs to Bolshevism.[28]

Moreover within months of writing these words Luxemburg was engaged in the most concrete form of practical solidarity with Lenin by participating in the foundation of the German Communist Party.[29]

Rosa Luxemburg was a thinker of great stature and independence. As such she inevitably differed with Lenin on many points of theory and tactics; but what she shared with Lenin—total commitment to revolutionary marxism and the international class struggle of the proletariat—was much more fundamental. They debated fiercely, yes, but within a shared framework, and not at all in the way that both of them fought Bernstein and the later Kautsky. Only on the basis of an understanding of this shared framework, their common starting point, can their disagreements on the nature and role of the party be properly grasped and estimated.

3. The background to Luxemburg's views

If, as we have argued, Lenin and Luxemburg started from the same fundamental premises, how then are their very real differences on the question of the party to be explained? Explanations in terms of Luxemburg's temperament do not get us very far. Whatever temperamental aversion she may have felt for Lenin's methods, she was a sufficiently disciplined revolutionary to have overcome her personal feelings had she thought it politically necessary, just as Trotsky did in 1917. Even less can they be attributed to any intellectual weakness on her part, for there was little exaggeration involved when Franz Mehring described her as: 'the most brilliant intellect of all the scientific heirs of Marx and Engels'.[30]

The real roots of Luxemburg's differences with Lenin lay in the very different historical situations in which they operated. Although both *Organisational Questions of Russian Social Democracy* and *The Mass Strike* took the Russian workers' movement as their subject, it is clear that Luxemburg wrote very much with an eye to the German situation and with the German experience in mind. In *The Mass Strike* this orientation is explicit, but even in the earlier work we find that when she wants a concrete example of the dangers of over-centralism and the conservative tendencies of leadership it is German Social Democracy and its adaptation to parliamentarianism that she cites.[31] Above all it was the German situation which shaped her conception of the party; and the conditions facing the German and Russian labour movements could hardly have been more dissimilar.

In the first place, on coming to Germany Luxemburg joined an already existing mass party—the largest and most successful socialist party the world had seen—with hundreds of thousands of members, thousands of local organisations, eighty or so daily papers and several decades of struggle behind it. Lenin, however, had to build up a party from scratch. Thus, whereas Lenin had to take very seriously all the practical (and therefore the theoretical) problems of organisation, efficiency and professionalism, Luxemburg could take all this for granted. Exactly how the party should be organised was never an issue in the SPD, and there is no evidence that she ever thought seriously about the details of organisation at all. In this respect the contrast with Lenin could not be more complete.

In the second place was the fact that both the SPD and their associated trade unions had already reached an advanced stage of bureaucratisation in what was the fatherland of bureaucracy and order. As we have already noted in this study, the German workers' movement sustained a huge layer of privileged and sedentary officials whose watchword 'organisation' served as a perennial alibi for avoiding action. Either the organisation was not yet strong enough for action or, alternatively, the action would jeopardise the organisations. This Rosa Luxemburg saw more clearly and earlier than any other marxist, certainly long before Lenin, and she reacted violently against it. It was in order to break through this great morass of conservative officialdom that she urged so forcefully the spontaneous creativity of the masses.

Moreover it was precisely spontaneity and struggle that were lacking in the German labour movement. The level of strike activity in the German working class in the first years of the century was very low. In the six years 1900 to 1905 there was an average of 1,171 strikes per year involving an average of 122,606 strikers per year (which puts the average number of workers per strike at only 104).[32] Compare this record with the figures for Russia where, with a very much smaller labour force, there were 87,000 strikers in 1903; 2,863,000 strikers in 1905 (1,843,000 of them involved in *political* strikes); and 550,000 *political* strikers in 1912.[33] From this it can be seen that the German workers' movement, for all its great socialist party and magnificent organisations, was relatively weak and passive in the elementary class struggle against the employers, while in Russia, where there was no mass party and where trade-union organisation was practically non-existent, the workers fought great battles against both the bosses and the state. It was in the nature of a revolutionary like Rosa Luxemburg, just as it was in the nature of Lenin, to put all the emphasis on what appeared to be the key *missing* element in the situation—which for her was spontaneity and mass action from below. Thus Lenin, taking spontaneity as given, could write; 'Give us an organisation of revolutionaries and we will overturn Russia', whereas Luxemburg said, in effect, 'Give us the spontaneity of the masses and we will have the revolution.'

In addition to these general factors, Luxemburg was also influenced by the specific situation within the SPD. The obvious first step towards building a genuine revolutionary party in Germany would have been the formation of a faction inside the SPD. But this would have been extremely difficult, for she would have had very little support for her views—even Lenin would not have supported such a venture before August 1914. The authority of the party's two great leaders, Kautsky as theoretician and Bebel as practical organiser, was immense—far greater than that of Plekhanov, the only comparable figure in Russia—and the influence that Luxemburg did have in the German movement she owed, at least in part, to their tolerance of her and to the fact that until 1910 she had the ear of Kautsky. What is more she needed an alliance with the centre of the party to combat the threat of Bernsteinism.

Finally, there was the fact that having a faction invariably raises the question of a split and this Rosa Luxemburg was completely against. It is possible that she was influenced in this by the fate of the Independent Socialist Party, quite a large group of revolutionaries who split from the SPD in 1891, accusing it of reformism. This had a very short life before completely disappearing. As late as January 1917 Luxemburg was still arguing against a split:

> However commendable and comprehensible the impatience and bitter-
> ness which leads so many of the best elements to leave the party today,
> a flight remains a flight. It is a betrayal of the masses who, sold to the
> bourgeoisie, writhe and choke from the stranglehold of Scheidemann and
> Legien. One may withdraw from small sects when they do not suit one
> any longer in order to found new sects. It is nothing more than immature
> fantasy to want to liberate the mass of the proletariat from this heavy
> and terrible yoke of the bourgeoisie by a simple withdrawal, and thus
> set a brave example. The discarding of membership cards as an illusion
> of liberation is nothing but the illusion, stood on its head, that power is
> inherent in a membership card. Both are different poles of organisational
> cretinism, the constitutional sickness of old German Social Democracy.[34]

4. The strengths and weaknesses of her position

We have shown how Luxemburg's emphasis on spontaneity and her conception of the role of the party were conditioned by her specific historical situation, but explanation is not justification. It is necessary also to make an assessment of her views in terms of their ability to solve the problems facing the working class in its struggle for power. We should begin by stating her merits, since her ideas have too frequently been dismissed by marxists simply on the authority of *What is to be done?*

Rosa Luxemburg was right that the most important advances in the field of tactics and methods of struggle of the proletariat are not invented by any central committee or leadership but are discovered and created by workers themselves in the heat of the battle. This has been demonstrated again and again, both on the grand scale with the spontaneous creation of a new type of state (the Paris Commune; the Russian soviets), and in a similar way with factory occupations and the innovation of the flying picket (British miners and building workers in 1972).

She was right that the class struggle in full flow does not allow the mechanical separation of the economic and the political, and her formulations on this question in *The Mass Strike* are far more dialectical than some of the abstract schemas in *What is to be done?* Again recent struggles of the British working class illustrate this admirably. The existence of the Tory Industrial Relations Act and the wages freeze in the early 1970s meant that purely trade-union, economic disputes such as the dockers' struggles against containerisation in 1972, the strike for trade-union recognition at the Con-Mech factory in 1973 and the miners' strike in 1974 inevitably transformed themselves into mass political battles against the law and the government. Indeed, since modern capitalist governments are today more and more compelled to intervene in industry and to make wage restraint the centre of their whole strategy, the political and economic struggle of the working class is more closely fused than ever and this aspect of Luxemburg's thought has become increasingly relevant.

Luxemburg was right to warn about the inherent conservative tendencies at the top of socialist parties and even in parties as a whole, which are produced by isolation from the dynamic forces at work unseen in the depths of the working class. Lenin himself, as we have seen, experienced this within the Bolshevik party both in 1905 and 1917. A contemporary marxist, Duncan Hallas, has explained clearly how this can happen even on the factory floor itself:

> It sometimes happens that even the best militants find themselves over-taken by events and occupying a position for a shorter or longer time, to the right of previously unmilitant workers. The experience is familiar to active rank-and-file trade unionists. Slogans and demands that were yes-terday acceptable only to the more conscious people can quite suddenly be too limited for the majority when a struggle develops beyond the expected point. Inevitably the greater experience and knowledge of the activists induces a certain caution, normally appropriate, but which, in a rapidly changing situation, can sometimes be a real barrier to advance.[35]

She was right also to oppose to Lenin's conception of the introduc-tion of socialism into the working class 'from without', the enormous role and achievements of spontaneity. The party is neither the fount of all wisdom nor the omnipotent managing director of the class struggle, and there is an element of truth in the charge that Lenin was bending the stick too far in the direction of voluntarism (though, as we have shown, this was also, in a sense, his great achievement).

Thus on a number of points Rosa Luxemburg was closer to a cor-rect marxist analysis than was the Lenin of 1901–04.[36] Unfortunately her conception also contained decisive weaknesses which were clearly exposed in the course of history. It is easy to see the one-sidedness of her views on the spontaneity of mass strikes. While such strikes can, and frequently do, break out spontaneously, this is not necessarily the case, nor is it always an advantage. The British General Strike of 1926 illus-trates this well. All the force, energy and initiative for the strike came from below, but the strike *was* planned and *was* called by the leadership, the General Council of the TUC, and most important it was effectively demobilised by that leadership at the crucial moment. In the months prior to the strike the British ruling class prepared very carefully, both politically and militarily, for the confrontation. Clearly in that situation marxist criticism would be directed not at the idea that the strike could be planned but against the General Council for failing to plan and pre-pare sufficiently when it was known that the enemy was doing so. But this was a relatively minor fault, which Luxemburg was easily capable of correcting.[37] Much more significant is the fact that her strategy failed the all important test of the German revolution itself.

In the long awaited German revolution of 1918–19 Rosa Luxemburg's Spartacus League (originally formed as a faction inside the SPD in 1916) proved itself to be the only consistently revolutionary force in Germany. Nonetheless it was too weak in numbers, experience and in organisational cohesiveness to decisively influence events. Rather it was continually blown about in the revolutionary gale unable to formulate a coherent strategy other than calling repeatedly for mass action and all power to the workers' and soldiers' councils. Radek, present as an emissary from Russia, reported that at the onset of the revolution the Spartacists had no more than fifty organised people in Berlin,[38] and even at the Conference at which the Spartacus League founded the German Communist Party, he felt moved to comment: 'I still did not feel that I was in the presence of a party.'[39]

Even Rosa Luxemburg's most ardent and uncritical supporter, Paul Frölich, confirms this picture of weakness (though he does not recognise its harmful effect on strategy): 'When the revolution came the Spartakusbund was only a federation of local groups existing in almost all the larger towns, and not yet a political party.'[40] In addition it suffered all the 'infantile disorders' of a youthful organisation. Luxemburg and the Executive were overruled by a substantial majority at the KPD founding conference on the question of participation in the elections to the National Assembly. (The Bolsheviks had disposed of this kind of ultra-leftism a decade before the test of 1917.) Unable to make a substantial impact within the workers' councils, the Spartacus League was forced into an unstable alliance with the USPD (Independent Social Democrats, who had split from the SPD in 1917) and the Revolutionary Shop Stewards, and then had to attempt to disentangle itself when the latter elements vacillated. In the end, despite the words of its own programme that: 'The Spartakusbund will never take over governmental power except in accordance with the clear and explicit will of the great majority of the proletarian masses in Germany',[41] it was overtaken by events and led into a hopelessly premature rising which resulted in the crushing of the revolution and the murder of Luxemburg and Liebknecht.

Luxemburg was undoubtedly aware of the mistakes that were being made, but was powerless to prevent them. Thus her failure to weld the advanced workers together in a disciplined independent vanguard party eventually cost her her life. That she had not begun this task as Lenin had in 1903 was due perhaps to unavoidable historical factors, but that it was not done later was in part a conscious decision. Nettl records that: 'The Spartacus leaders deliberately decided to forego any sustained attempt to create an organisation in 1918. They held that the revolutionary possibilities made this an unnecessary dispersal of effort.'[42]

The other great defect in Luxemburg's strategy was her underestimation of the ability of reformist leaders to hold back and disorient the working class. Although she was the first to perceive the theoretical implications of Bernsteinism and the passivity of the Kautskyite centre, she nonetheless failed to foresee the paralysing and divisive effect these tendencies would have on the working class even in the midst of the mass actions she longed for. In 1913 she wrote: 'Leaders who hang back will certainly be pushed aside by the storming masses.'[43]

But in reality this did not prove so simple. Instead the social democrats were able to exploit the long-established allegiance of millions of workers to sabotage the revolution. It was because of her failure to grasp this problem early enough that Luxemburg did not see the need to combat opportunism organisationally—that is, by clauses in the party constitution, by splitting etc.—as well as by political debate.

5. The theoretical roots of her errors

We have already indicated the background to Luxemburg's views and one can see how both the strengths and weaknesses of her position were historically conditioned. But what of the theoretical roots of her errors? We must turn for the source of these mistakes to two interrelated areas of her thought: her analysis of the process by which the proletariat develops its revolutionary consciousness, and her conception of the dynamics of the revolution itself.

For the mainstream of social democracy consciousness was seen as developing through a harmonious process of gradual accumulation without contradictions and without qualitative leaps. Luxemburg's emphasis on the spontaneity of the masses placed her furthest of all the western marxists from this orthodox view, but she still did not break the circle completely. It was not that she over-estimated the heights to which workers could spontaneously rise but that she overestimated the *evenness* with which this process could occur. Clearly she recognised that some workers are more capable and courageous than others and that some have a higher level of socialist consciousness than others. What she did not fully comprehend was that between the revolutionary worker who wishes to overthrow capitalism and the less advanced worker who wishes to improve his conditions within capitalism there exists a certain contradiction (albeit not an insoluble one); and that on the basis of this contradiction there arise parties claiming to be parties of the working class, but which actually operate as bourgeois agents within the labour movement.

It was because of this gap in her theory that she failed to see the necessity of organising the advanced revolutionary workers separately and independently so as to increase their influence within the class as a whole, and to equip them for struggle against opportunist and reformist influences on the class. Her underestimation of the negative effects of bad leaders also derives from this source. For if the working class radicalised not only spontaneously but also *uniformly*, then indeed 'leaders who hung back would be pushed aside by storming masses'.[44]

As for Luxemburg's concept of the revolution, a comment by Tony Cliff can serve as our starting point:

> The main reason for Rosa Luxemburg's overestimation of the factor of spontaneity and underestimation of the factor of organisation probably lies in the need, in the *immediate* struggle against reformism, for emphasis on spontaneity as the *first* step in all revolutions. From this one stage in the struggle of the proletariat she generalised too widely to embrace the struggle as a whole.[45]

We can further develop this by saying that Luxemburg tended to identify the mass strike (which frequently coincides with the spontaneous outbreak of revolutions) with the climax of the revolution itself. In *The Mass Strike* she wrote as follows:

> Today when the working classes are being enlightened in the cause of the revolutionary struggles, when they must marshal their forces and lead themselves, and when the revolution is directed as much against the old state power as against capitalist exploitation, the mass strike appears as the natural means of recruiting the widest proletarian layers for the struggle, as well as being at the same time a means of undermining and overthrowing the old state power and of stemming capitalist exploitation . . .
>
> The chief form of previous bourgeois revolutions, the fight at the barricades, the open conflict with the armed power of the state, is in the revolution of today, only the culminating point, only a moment in the process of the proletarian class struggle.[46]

But in fact the general strike, whatever its size, strength and militancy, merely raises the question of power—it does not and cannot resolve it. Only the destruction of the old state power through insurrection can do that. And insurrection must, by its very nature, be organised: it must be a unified, simultaneous action of decisive sections of the proletariat, prepared in advance and in secret and set for a definite date. Its execution demands, therefore, a well established chain of command with influence and authority extending throughout the class. In other words the insurrection, as was shown by our analysis of the October Revolution in Chapter 3, can be organised successfully only by the party—and not just any kind of party, but a disciplined combat party capable of moving as one.

It would not be true to say that Rosa Luxemburg never considered the question of insurrection (she wrote a small pamphlet on it in January 1906[47]) but it is mentioned only incidentally in *The Mass Strike* and there is no evidence that she ever faced the problem squarely or thought through its implications for the nature of the party. Had she done so, she would have been forced to revise her propagandistic conception of the role of the party (for it is precisely with the insurrection that the balance between propaganda and action in the work of the party shifts decisively in favour of the latter) and also her views on discipline and centralism. Lenin, by contrast, had related the nature of his organisation to the seizure of power from the beginning.

The problem of the insurrection and the party is also related to the unevenness in the consciousness of the proletariat in a way that is particularly relevant to the fate of Rosa Luxemburg in the German Revolution. The opposite side of the same coin, which causes some sections of the class to lag behind others (and to continue to adhere to reformist parties), is the impulse the revolution gives to the advanced workers to attempt to seize power prematurely. Exactly this occurred in the Russian Revolution with the 'July Days' and in the German Revolution with the January Rioting. In Russia, as we noted in Chapter 3, the Bolsheviks were able to clearly oppose the adventure, prevent it doing too much damage, preserve their organisation and prepare for the next round in the battle. In Germany the Spartacus League was swept along by events to disaster. The difference lay, not in Lenin's 'intelligence' or 'realism', as against Rosa Luxemburg's 'revolutionary romanticism', but in the existence in Russia of a hardened party with authority among the advanced workers and its absence in Germany.

6. Marx, Lenin and Luxemburg

The reference points for any overall judgement of Rosa Luxemburg's theory of the party must necessarily be Marx and Lenin. In many respects Luxemburg was closer to Marx than was Lenin. She shared Marx's strengths, his opposition to sectarianism and his emphasis on the mass activity of the working class. She also shared his weakness: an over-optimistic and foreshortened view of the process by which the class-in-itself transforms itself into a class-for-itself—the assumption that the objective economic unity of the working class would spontaneously lead to its ultimate political unity. Consequently she shared with Marx a certain tendency toward fatalism in the sphere of organisation. We have already noted that against Lenin she was not entirely in the wrong in the polemics of 1904, but Lenin was able, through the experience of 1905, to correct the onesidedness of his early formulations and so make good his decisive advance over Marx, whereas Rosa Luxemburg was not. Had she lived to assimilate and reflect on the experience of the German Revolution, it is possible, indeed probable, that she would have achieved this correction.

As it stands Rosa Luxemburg's theory of the party and its relationship to the working class remains a useful weapon in a labour movement which, throughout the world, has suffered decades of bureaucratic domination by social democracy and Stalinism alike. But ultimately it is a useful weapon only insofar as it is integrated into the framework of Leninism. As an *alternative* to Leninism, Luxemburgism must be judged invalid.

5.
Trotsky's dual legacy

There are two aspects to Trotsky's contribution to the marxist theory of the revolutionary party. First, there is his defence, principally through the medium of the Left Opposition, of the Leninist conception of the party against the practical and theoretical assault mounted on it by Stalin and the Stalinist bureaucracy. Secondly, there is his attempt, culminating in the foundation of the Fourth International, to forge a genuine marxist alternative to the degenerated Communist International. Although, of course, there is continuity between these two aspects in that the latter grew logically out of the former, there is nonetheless a qualitative difference between them. At the period of the Left Opposition, Trotsky counterposed to Stalin's opportunist policy a consistent revolutionary one. With the effort to build a Fourth International, Trotsky now had to embody his policy in an organisation of his own. Because of this difference it makes sense to divide our study of Trotsky's theory of the party into two parts: the defence of Leninism; and the Fourth International.

A. The Defence of Leninism
Trotsky divided from Stalin and the official majority of the CPSU over two basic issues: the bureaucratic degeneration of the Russian state and the Stalinist theory of 'socialism in one country'. The two issues were naturally connected. The bureaucracy arose by the exhaustion and dispersal of the revolutionary proletariat as a result of the cumulative sufferings of the first world war and civil war and the accompanying economic devastation, famine, epidemics and physical annihilation.[1] This bureaucracy, consisting in large part of careerists, administrators taken over from the old regime, ex-Mensheviks and long declassed workers, wanted above all an end to upheavals and to carry on business-as-usual. They had no interest in what seemed to them the romantic and

dangerous adventure of world revolution. Thus the theory of socialism in one country was not a mere Stalinist invention. On the contrary, 'it expressed unmistakeably the mood of the bureaucracy. When speaking of the victory of socialism, they meant their own victory.'[2]

This then was a dispute over fundamentals, as deep as the split between communism and social democracy. It involved two completely different and opposed conceptions of socialism. For Trotsky, as for Marx and Lenin, socialism was a classless, stateless, self-governing community based on an abundance of material goods, in which 'the free development of each is the condition for the free development of all'[3]. Dictatorship, state planning, economic growth and efficiency, iron discipline etc. were means to this end (means from which Trotsky did not shrink), but not ends in themselves. For Stalin, as for the bureaucracy of which he was the prime representative, socialism was identified precisely with nationalisation, state control and the economic and military growth of Russia into a front-rank world power. From Trotsky's point of view, a degree of bureaucratisation was perhaps unavoidable, but it remained an ever-present danger to be closely watched and dispensed with as soon as possible. From Stalin's, it was the essential core and foundation of a new regime. Given Trotsky's conception of socialism, the prospect of its realisation in one country—and backward Russia at that—was a reactionary utopia. Given Stalin's, it was the only practical and realistic perspective.

Being a dispute about fundamentals, this conflict necessarily expanded to the point where it affected every event and every policy in the life of the international working-class movement, including of course the nature, role, strategy and tactics of the revolutionary party and the revolutionary international. Trotsky's disputes with Stalin over the Leninist theory of the party can, for clarity, be dealt with under two headings: party democracy in the CPSU, and the strategy of the international communist parties.

1. Party democracy

The gradual bureaucratisation of the Soviet state in the absence of an energetic and politically active working class necessarily raised the question of the bureaucratisation of the Communist Party and the destruction of its inner party democracy. For although there was a formal separation between state (soviet) and party institutions, the Bolsheviks constituted in reality a state party. Since the civil war the party had maintained a complete political monopoly and control over all key posts. Consequently if the state machine was becoming bureaucratised, it could not fail also to have an effect on the party. What made this so crucial was that the party, as the vanguard of the proletariat with its core of incorruptible old Bolsheviks, its revolutionary tradition, its maximum earnings rule[4] and its strict discipline, was generally regarded as the main bulwark against bureaucracy. If the party succumbed, there would, given the passivity of the workers, be no further line of defence. It was in 1923 that Trotsky felt the situation had become so serious that he had to launch an open struggle for democracy within the party, with a series of articles for *Pravda* entitled collectively *The New Course*.[5]

The tone of *The New Course* is cautious and some of the formulations are hesitant, but in many respects it is an admirable presentation of the case for democracy within the revolutionary party and is of lasting value. Trotsky does not pose the question of democracy as an abstract right but locates its necessity in the development of the party and the new historical stage being entered. First, he examines relations between the old and new generation (pre- and post-October) of party members: 'The conquest of power was followed by a rapid, even abnormal, growth of the party.'[6] There was an influx both of inexperienced workers with little consciousness and of certain alien elements, functionaries and hangers-on. 'In this chaotic period [the party] was able to preserve its Bolshevist nature only thanks to the internal dictatorship of the old guard, which had been tested in October.'[7]

But since then the situation had changed. Now the new generation, for the sake of its own political development and for the future of the party as a whole, must be drawn actively into the political life and decision-making process of the party. Then Trotsky looks at the social composition of the party, showing how the need to fill administrative posts with workers led to the weakening of 'its fundamental cells, the factory nuclei',[8] and this was an important source of bureaucratism. Trotsky argues for the necessity of strengthening the proletarian base of the party and for the use of the students and youth as a force against bureaucracy.

On the necessity of internal democracy Trotsky writes:

The essential incomparable advantage of our party consists in its being able, at every moment, to look at industry with the eyes of the communist machinist, the communist specialist, the communist director, and the communist merchant, collect the experience of these mutually complementary workers, draw conclusions from them, and thus determine its line for directing economy in general and each enterprise in particular. It is clear that such leadership is reliable only on the basis of a vibrant and active democracy inside the party.[9]

These remarks are directed to a party in power and in a specific situation, but the principle contained in them, the necessity of democracy for correct leadership, is of general validity.

The main burden of the leadership's answer to Trotsky's criticism was an outraged defence of the great traditions of the old guard and an emphasis on the imperative need for party unity and the dangers of factionalism. Trotsky's reply points out that 'tradition' has a negative as well as a positive side in the revolutionary movement. Citing numerous examples, including the stand of the Old Bolsheviks against Lenin's "April Theses," he argues that Bolshevism's 'most precious fundamental tactical quality is its unequalled aptitude to orient itself rapidly, to change tactics quickly, to renew its armament and to apply new methods, in a word, to carry out abrupt turns,'[10] and that no tradition, however revolutionary, in itself provides infallible supra-historical guarantees against degeneration. On the question of factions Trotsky recognises the great danger of factionalism in the situation, and the possibility that factional differences may rapidly come to reflect the pressure of social and class forces hostile to the proletariat, but contends that an undemocratic party regime is in itself a cause of factionalism.

> The leading organs of the party must lend an ear to the voice of the broad party mass, not consider every criticism as a manifestation of factional spirit, and thereby drive conscientious and disciplined communists to maintain a systematic silence or else constitute themselves as factions.[11]

The essence of Trotsky's case in *The New Course* is that

> it is in contradictions and differences of opinion that the working out of the party's public opinion inevitably takes place. To localise this process only within the apparatus which is then charged to furnish the party with the fruit of its labours in the form of slogans, orders etc. is to sterilise the party ideologically and politically.[12]

At the same time, the claims of authority in the immensely difficult objective situation still exercise a strong hold over Trotsky. While demanding inner-party democracy he nonetheless accepts that 'We are the only party in the country and, in the period of the dictatorship, it could not be otherwise.'[13] And in so doing Trotsky participated in the current practice of raising to the level of a general principle what was originally envisaged as a merely temporary measure due to the extraordinary situation of the civil war. Max Shachtman, an erstwhile follower of Trotsky, sees in this a fundamental contradiction.

> Trotsky . . . gave no sign of realising . . . that the denial of democratic rights to those outside the party could be enforced only by the denial, sooner or later, of the same rights to the members of that very party itself. For this is a veritable law of politics; every serious difference of opinion in a serious political party entails an appeal—direct or indirect, explicit or implicit, deliberate or unintentioned—to one or other segment of the people outside this party.[14]

This is a substantial point, but it does not really undermine Trotsky's whole position. There is no doubt that in the long run, 'sooner or later', dictatorship by one party will lead to dictatorship within the party, but, as Trotsky often says, in politics time is an important factor. From Trotsky's point of view the Bolsheviks were engaged in an exceptionally difficult and delicate holding operation: between 'sooner' and 'later' there was the possibility of relief from the international revolution.

As Stalin extended his despotic control over the party and the country and as his policy diverged ever further from revolutionary marxism, so the calls for party democracy became more insistent and opposition to Stalin's organisational methods became irreconcilable.

The 1927 *Platform of the Joint Opposition* signed by Trotsky, Zinoviev and eleven other members of the Central Committee contains a ringing indictment of the party regime:

> The last few years have seen a systematic abolition of inner-party democracy—in violation of the whole tradition of the Bolshevik party, in violation of the direct decisions of a series of party congresses. The genuine election of officials is in actual practice dying out. The organisational principles of Bolshevism are being perverted at every step. The party constitution is being systematically changed, to increase the volume of rights at the top, and diminish the rights of the branches at the bottom.

The leadership of the regional committees, the regional executive committees, the regional trade union councils etc. are, in actual fact, irremovable . . . The right of each member of the party, of each group of party members, to 'appeal its radical differences to the court of the whole party', [Lenin] is in actual fact annulled. Congresses and conferences are called without a preliminary free discussion (such as was always held under Lenin) of all questions by the whole party. The demand for such a discussion is treated as a violation of party discipline . . .

The dying out of inner-party democracy leads to a dying out of workers' democracy in general—in the trade unions, and in all other non-party mass organisations.[15]

In this *Platform*, the analysis, warnings and suggestions of *The New Course* have crystallised into programmatic demands: prepare for the fifteenth congress upon a basis of real inner-party democracy; every comrade and group of comrades to have an opportunity to defend their point of view before the party; improve the social composition by admitting into the party only workers from the factories and the land; proletarianise and cut down the party apparatus; reinstate immediately the expelled Oppositionists; reconstruct the Central Control Committee independently of the apparatus. But at this stage the condemnation and the demands still operate within the framework of complete loyalty to the Russian Communist Party and acceptance of its political monopoly.

We will struggle with all our force against the formation of two parties, for the dictatorship of the proletariat demands as its very core a single proletarian party.[16]

By 1933, after the paralysis of the Comintern in the face of Hitler (see below) and the total liquidation of all opposition and criticism in Russia, Trotsky abandoned this last constraint. Declaring that the Bolshevik Party of Lenin had been completely destroyed by Stalinism, he called for the building of revolutionary parties anew and the over-throw of the bureaucracy by political revolution. In 1936 in his major work *The Revolution Betrayed*, Trotsky was able to make a completely unequivocal exposition of his views on party democracy.

The inner regime of the Bolshevik party was characterised by the method of *democratic centralism*. The combination of these two concepts, democracy and centralism, is not in the least contradictory. The party took watchful care not only that its boundaries should always be strictly defined, but also that all those who entered these boundaries should enjoy the actual right to define the direction of the party policy. Freedom of criticism and intellectual struggle was an irrevocable content of the party democracy. The present doctrine that Bolshevism does not tolerate factions is a myth of the epoch of decline. In reality the history of Bolshevism is a history of the struggle of factions. And, indeed, how could a genuinely revolutionary organisation, setting itself the task of overthrowing the world and uniting under its banner the most audacious iconoclasts, fighters and insurgents, live and develop without intellectual conflicts, without groupings and temporary factional formations? The farsightedness of the Bolshevik leadership often made it possible to soften conflicts and shorten the duration of factional struggle, but no more than that. The Central Committee relied upon this seething democratic support. From this it derived the audacity to make decisions and give orders. The obvious correctness of the leadership at all critical stages gave it that high authority which is the priceless moral capital of centralism.

The regime of the Bolshevik party, especially before it came to power, stood thus in complete contradiction to the regime of the present sections of the Communist International, with their 'leaders' appointed from above, making complete changes of policy at a word of command, with their uncontrolled apparatus, haughty in its attitude to the rank and file, servile in its attitude to the Kremlin.[17]

Trotsky not only restores the original Bolshevik position on factions but also breaks with the doctrine of the one-party state.

In the beginning the party had wished and hoped to preserve freedom of political struggle within the framework of the soviets. The civil war introduced stern amendments into this calculation. The opposition parties were forbidden one after another. This measure, obviously in conflict with the spirit of soviet democracy, the leaders of Bolshevism regarded not as a principle but as an episodic act of self-defence.[18]

He rejects the identification of class dictatorship with party dictatorship.

Since a class has many 'parts'—some look forward and some back—one and the same class may create several parties. For the same reason one party may rest upon parts of different classes. An example of only one party corresponding to one class is not to be found in the whole course of political history—provided, of course, you do not take the police appearance for the reality.[19]

And the 1938 programme of the Fourth International states that 'Democratisation of the soviets is impossible without *legalisation of soviet parties*. The workers and peasants themselves by their own free vote will indicate what parties they recognise as soviet parties.'[20]

When one surveys the record of Trotsky's struggle for workers' democracy in the Russian Communist Party and the Russian state, it is clear that he made many mistakes. With the benefit of hindsight one can say that he should have begun his resistance earlier, that there were times when he made a virtue out of necessity, that in 1923–24 he should have fought more energetically and consistently, that he should have appealed sooner to the rank-and-file of the party and sooner to the mass of workers themselves. Many of these criticisms may be justified, but they are also one-sided for they neglect the immense difficulties of the situation which Trotsky faced, in particular the deep passivity of the Russian workers, including the mass of party members, during this period. Also Trotsky clearly considered it the duty of revolutionaries, in the absence of any existing alternative, to remain loyal to the party of the revolution to the last possible moment. This was a weighty consideration, much easier to dismiss when the degeneration has run its course than in the midst of the struggle. A balanced view must recognise the immense achievement of Trotsky in defending and preserving the marxist and Leninist tradition of party democracy, of the party as a collective and living organism, against enormous odds, without collapsing, as did so many others, into either social-democratic or anarchist rejection of democratic centralism and the vanguard party.

2. The strategy of the international Communist Parties

The theory of socialism in one country was first proclaimed by Stalin in autumn 1924 in complete violation of all the traditions of marxism. Its most immediate effects were not on Russia itself but on the Communist International and the strategy of communist parties throughout the world. As long as the survival of the Russian Revolution was linked to the achievement of world revolution, the most concrete form of solidarity with Russia and the first duty of every 'foreign' party was to make the revolution in its own country. But once the building of socialism was held to be possible in Russia alone, the world revolution became not a necessity but an optional extra, and the role of the Comintern, in the eyes of Moscow, became to ensure that nothing untoward interrupted this process of 'socialist' construction. In this way the CPs were transformed from agents of working-class revolution into agents of the foreign policy of the Russian bureaucracy. This transformation inevitably meant a series of departures from and revisions of Leninist traditions of revolutionary politics. The principal defender of those traditions was Leon Trotsky.[21]

It is impossible to deal here with all the questions of party strategy on which Trotsky clashed with Stalin, but four examples will serve to illustrate Trotsky's contribution to the theory of the party in this sphere.

Trotsky opposed from the beginning Stalin's policy that the Chinese CP should subordinate itself to the bourgeois nationalist Kuomintang, which led to the bloody defeat of the Chinese revolution in 1927. He insisted throughout on the Leninist principle of the complete organisational and political independence of the revolutionary party.

Equally he opposed the collaboration with the TUC leadership through the Anglo-Soviet Trade Union Committee which fatally compromised the independence of the British CP and left it uncritical of the 'left' trade-union leaders who betrayed the General Strike.

Trotsky also mounted a brilliant and prophetic critique of Stalinist policy in Germany in 1929–33. The KPD, operating with Stalin's theory of 'social fascism', treated the social democrats as the main enemy and played down the threat of fascism. Against this disastrous strategy Trotsky insisted on the urgent need for a united front of working-class parties against Hitler.

Finally Trotsky demonstrated the fatal weakness of the Popular Front strategy adopted in 1934 which tied the working class and its party to the bourgeoisie and led to further defeats in Spain and France.[22] This critique is especially relevant today, as some variation of popular frontism is now the policy of almost every CP throughout the world and we have recently seen repeated its full tragic consequences in Chile.

Taken as a whole, the Stalinist period constituted a sustained perversion and distortion of the Leninist theory of the party to the point where it was transformed into its opposite. From a theory of the selection and organisation of the revolutionary vanguard of the proletariat, it became a myth of infallibility serving to justify every form of bureaucratic manipulation and cynical betrayal. So successful was this operation that Leninist and Stalinist theories of the party, so different in practice, became generally identified as one and the same in the eyes of the public. Were it not for the tireless work of Trotsky, this identification may well have passed effectively unchallenged in the marxist movement and genuine Leninism been completely buried under a mountain of lies.

B. The Fourth International

Trotsky's defence of the Leninist theory of the party as an integral part of his defence of marxism and Leninism as a whole was an immense achievement, but not one with which he could rest content. Since the turn of the century he had been committed to international proletarian revolution, and once he was convinced that the Stalinised Communist International could no longer achieve that end, he had no choice but to attempt to build a new organisation himself. It was the total collapse of the KPD before Hitler and the failure of a single section of the Comintern to protest at the official line which finally decided Trotsky to take this course.

> An organisation which was not roused by the thunder of fascism and which submits docilely to such outrageous acts of bureaucracy demonstrates thereby that it is dead and cannot be revived.[23]

Just as Lenin, after the capitulation of the Second International on 4 August 1914, immediately declared for a Third International, so Trotsky in 1933 issued the call for the Fourth International.

1. The struggle for the Fourth International

Trotsky's support in 1933 was very limited, and there could be no question of immediately setting up the new international. Instead it would have to be built gradually. Unfortunately the objective circumstances for doing this were extremely unfavourable. Lenin, although extremely isolated at the beginning of the first world war, had at least the advantage of a solid national base in the shape of the Bolshevik party. Even so it was not until two years after the victory of the Russian Revolution that the Third International could be founded. Trotsky had no such base, nor was he destined to see a second victory of the proletarian revolution in his lifetime. On the contrary, the 1930s were a period of profound defeats for the working class, beginning with the crushing of the German proletariat (the most total and shameful defeat of a militant, politically-conscious working class in history). Fascist or similar regimes already gripped the centre of Europe, and then followed the triumph of Franco in Spain. Meanwhile, throughout the thirties, the depression and long-term unemployment sapped the fighting strength and weakened the organisations of workers everywhere.

In addition to this general picture of black reaction, there were certain specific factors which worked against the growth of Trotskyism. The terrible threat of fascism created an immense pressure among workers for the closing of ranks, for unity in the face of the enemy and against new splits. Combined with this pressure for unity was the feeling of the need to have some ally, some great military power to stand against Hitler, and this of course meant Soviet Russia. To abandon the might of Stalin for the miniscule forces of Trotskyism was difficult in the extreme. In this way Hitler actually aided Stalin and Stalinism within the labour movement.

Then there was the fact that Trotsky was subjected to historically unprecedented vilification and slander within the working-class movement. The charge that Trotsky and all the other defendants in the Moscow Trials were agents of Hitler and the Mikado is and was manifestly absurd, and yet the power of 'the big lie' was such that millions of people throughout the world believed it. Nor was it just hardened communists who accepted the Trotsky fascist slander. Many Western artists and intellectuals, exemplified by Romain Rolland, lent their voices to the charge. Others such as Bernard Shaw or André Malraux, feeling the pressure of the popular front, equivocated or remained silent. Thus Stalin's great frame-up was, in the short term, highly successful. In the first place, it ensured that only those of considerable strength of character, capable of withstanding constant denunciation and obloquy, would adhere to Trotskyism. Secondly, it created an enormous barrier between the Trotskyists, including those with the most exemplary revolutionary records, and the politically-conscious workers, depriving them of an honest hearing for their case. Criticism, no matter how well argued, is unlikely to be heeded if it is believed that it comes from a 'fascist agent'.

Finally there was the simple fact that it was exceedingly hard to persuade people that it was necessary to begin all over again so soon after the establishment of the Third International. Trotsky expressed the situation as follows:

> We are not progressing politically. Yes it is a fact which is an expression
> of a general decay of the workers' movements in the last fifteen years . . .
> Our situation now is incomparably more difficult than that of any other
> organisation at any other time, because we have the terrible betrayal of

the Second International. The degeneration of the Third International developed so quickly and so unexpectedly that the same generation which heard its formation now hears us and they say 'But we have already heard this once'.[24]

The effect of this appallingly difficult situation was that the Trotskyist movement was stamped with three characteristics. Firstly it was extremely small, consisting in many countries of mere handfuls. Secondly it was overwhelmingly petty-bourgeois in social composition. Thirdly it was, at least in its upper ranks, an organisation of exiles—not necessarily exiles from their countries, though this was true of some, but exiles from their adopted homeland, the mass workers' movement. Now small groups always split more easily and more often than large parties, for there is so much less to lose. Petty-bourgeois intellectuals are always more prone to factionalism than are workers. 'All the people of this type' wrote the American Trotskyist leader, J. P. Cannon, 'have one common characteristic: they like to discuss things without limit or end.'[25] And exile politics is notorious for its intrigue and scandal. At bottom these phenomena all have the same cause—isolation from the great disciplinary force of the class struggle—and the movement for the Fourth International suffered grievously from all of them. From the beginning Trotskyism was plagued by factionalism, splits and extreme sectarianism.

Trotsky fought as best he could to break out of this hopeless milieu and to find a way for his movement to reach the workers. At first he orientated his followers towards the various left, social-democratic and centrist groups (such as the British ILP and the German Socialist Workers' Party) which were independent of the Second and Third Internationals, in the hope that this could constitute a new Zimmerwald.[26] Then he directed them towards short-term entry into the mass social-democratic parties,[27] and led them out again. In 1937 and again in 1939 Trotsky proposed to the American Socialist Workers' Party the expulsion of petty-bourgeois members who failed to recruit workers to the party.[28] But it was all to no avail. Each new tactic caused new splits and each failed to achieve its aim. The Trotskyist movement never succeeded either in recruiting a substantial number of workers or in becoming an integrated part of the labour movement.

The question that we must now ask is: what was the effect of these conditions on Trotsky's theory of the party? For although it is possible for the theoretician to resist the demoralising impact of unfavourable events by holding firm to the theoretical acquisitions of the past and to the previous high points of the movement, as Lenin did during the Stolypin reaction in Russia, and as Trotsky did later, nonetheless it is impossible for theory to be totally unaffected by practice. So it was for Trotsky. The yawning gap between the enormous demands of the situation and the pathetically weak forces with which he could set about meeting them led Trotsky into not only an exaggeration of the viability and strength of his tiny organisation. He was also misled in his theoretical overestimation of the role that could be played by an international leadership divorced from the masses and in the substitution of the party programme, drawn up from the sidelines of the class struggle, for the party itself as the embodiment of the actual vanguard of the proletariat, and the generaliser of the experiences of the working class in the midst of great events. These points can best be illustrated by examining the decision taken in 1938 to actually found the Fourth International and the perspectives that accompanied it.

2. The theoretical basis of the Fourth International

The most immediately striking feature of the Fourth International was the contrast it presented with the first three workers' Internationals. The founding conference was a pitiful gathering compared with those of its predecessors. Held secretly in France in the home of Trotsky's old friend Alfred Rosmer, the conference lasted only a day and was attended by only 21 delegates. These delegates claimed to represent organisations in 11 countries, but most of these organisations were the tiniest of sectlets and one, the so-called 'Russian section', was a complete fiction and represented by a GPU agent (Etienne). Only Max Shachtman, the American delegate, came from a section with more than a couple of hundred members. In 1935 Trotsky had denounced as 'a stupid piece of gossip' the idea that 'the Trotskyists want to proclaim the Fourth International next Thursday'.[29] Why then, despite the fact that there had been no significant growth in his movement, did Trotsky nonetheless go ahead with this proclamation?

The answer lies in Trotsky's theory of the 'crisis of leadership' of the proletariat. It was Trotsky's conviction that both capitalism and Stalinism had reached an impossible impasse. The successful resolution of this crisis for all humanity depended entirely on the emergence of a new revolutionary leadership. In the inevitably approaching revolutionary situations the crucial factor would be the quality of the revolutionary leadership, and equally in such situations it would be possible for initially tiny organisations to rapidly gain a mass following and exercise a decisive influence on events.

The programme adopted at the founding conference, *The Death Agony of Capitalism and the Tasks of the Fourth International*, opens as follows:

> The world political situation as a whole is chiefly characterised by a historical crisis of the leadership of the proletariat . . . The objective prerequisites for the proletarian revolution have not only 'ripened'; they have begun to get somewhat rotten. Without a socialist revolution, in the next historical period at that, a catastrophe threatens the whole culture of mankind. The turn is now to the proletariat, i.e. chiefly to its revolutionary vanguard. The historical crisis of mankind is reduced to the crisis of the revolutionary leadership.[30]

The 'crisis of leadership' theory was a distillation of the revolutionary experience of a whole epoch, from the positive example of October 1917 through the negative examples of Hungary 1919, Italy 1920, Germany 1923 and 1933, China 1925–27 and Spain 1931–37. But this 'general' correctness of the theory does not exhaust the problem. Trotsky never for one moment claimed that the leadership created or 'made' the revolution (as for example some Guevarists have suggested), merely that it was a decisive 'link' in the chain of events, the other primary components of the chain being the objective economic and political crisis of capitalism, the mass upsurge of the working class and the existence of a well prepared revolutionary party. But without this chain 'the leadership' would be isolated, suspended in a vacuum and relatively impotent, and its position would be worse insofar as it had an inflated or false picture of its own capabilities and significance. The problem for Trotsky was that when in September 1938 he founded the Fourth International (World Party of the Socialist Revolution), vital links in the chain did not exist. There was neither an upsurge of the working class nor anywhere in the world a solidly-based revolutionary party.

Trotsky was naturally acutely aware of this. He 'solved' the problem by a series of predictions in which he forecast the inevitable emergence of the component links in the revolutionary chain in the near future.

Firstly, he believed that capitalism had entered its final crisis. 'The economic prerequisite for the proletarian revolution has already in general achieved the highest point of fruition that can be reached under capitalism. Mankind's productive forces stagnate.'[31] The situation was such that there could be 'no discussion of systematic social reforms and raising of the masses' living standards',[32] as a consequence of which social democracy would be fatally undermined.

Secondly, he saw the approaching world war as unleashing, like its predecessor only more so, an enormous revolutionary wave: 'Second births are commonly easier than first. In the new war, it will not be necessary to wait a whole two years and a half for the first insurrection.'[33]

Thirdly, he believed the Stalinist regime in Russia to be highly unstable—'like a pyramid balanced on its head'—and unable to withstand the shock of war. 'If it is not paralysed by revolution in the West, imperialism will sweep away the regime which issued from the October revolution.'[34] And while Trotsky was for the defence of the Soviet Union, he could not fail to reckon with the fact that such an overthrow would deal a fatal blow to what he regarded as the main counter-revolutionary force in the workers' movement.

Fourthly, in line with Lenin's *Imperialism* and his own theory of permanent revolution, he thought that the colonies would be unable to gain independence without a head-on conflict with imperialism, and, since the national bourgeoisies would shrink from this conflict, the rising national liberation movements would have to take the road of socialist revolution. 'The banner on which is emblazoned the struggle for the liberation of the colonial and semi-colonial peoples, i.e. a good half of mankind, has definitely passed into the hands of the Fourth International.'[35]

Taken as a whole this amounted to a perspective in which

The epoch . . . about to begin for European humanity will not leave a trace in the labour movement of all that is ambiguous and gangrened . . . The sections of the Second and Third Internationals will depart the scene without a sound, one after the other. A new and grand regrouping of the workers' ranks is inevitable. The young revolutionary cadres will acquire flesh and blood.[36]

For each of the predictions that made up this perspective there was much evidence, but the fact remains that every one of them was falsified by history. Preparations for the war began to lift capitalism out of the slump, and the ultimate crisis of the system diagnosed by Trotsky turned after the war into the system's most sustained and spectacular boom. Stalin's regime did not collapse in the war but emerged victorious and greatly strengthened, extending its control over the whole of Eastern Europe.[37] Far from 'departing the scene without a sound,' the social-democratic and communist parties gained, on the basis of these developments, a new lease of life throughout Europe. Imperialism was able, for the most part, to grant independence to the colonies through a deal with the colonial bourgeoisies, thus severing the connection between national liberation and proletarian revolution. The Fourth International was thus left high and dry.

Trotsky had predicted:

> During the next ten years the programme of the Fourth International will become the guide of millions and these revolutionary millions will know how to storm heaven and earth.[38]

But when, ten years later in 1948, the Second World Congress of the Fourth International was convened, it still represented only tiny groups.

The falsification of Trotsky's predictions rendered his abstractly correct theory of 'crisis of leadership' irrelevant for practical purposes. But let us assume that the perspective, in its essentials, had proved correct; would all then have been well? Would the tiny Fourth International have been able to assume leadership of the unfolding world revolutionary process confidently and guide it to victory? Of course such a question, like all historical 'might-have-beens', is strictly speaking unanswerable, but it is clear that at least two major problems, deriving from the decision to found the International, would have arisen.

Firstly, the Trotskyist groups were so small and weak (much weaker than, for example, the Bolsheviks as early as 1903, or the Spartacists in 1914, or Trotsky's Mezhrayontsy group in 1917)[39] that it would have been very hard for them to make themselves felt in the midst of a great revolutionary upheaval. A small party, it is true, can grow amazingly in time of revolution, but unless it possesses at the outset at least a certain size and viability, it is likely to be overwhelmed by events. This is the point of the long labour of party-building in the pre-revolutionary period. Trotsky hoped to overcome this difficulty by means of a system of 'transitional demands' which would enable the small group to relate to and spearhead the struggle of the masses. He wrote:

> The strategic task of the next period . . . consists in overcoming the contradiction between the maturity of the objective revolutionary conditions and the immaturity of the proletariat and its vanguard . . . It is necessary to help the masses in the process of the daily struggle to find the bridge between present demands and the socialist programme of the revolution. This bridge should include a system of transitional demands, stemming from today's conditions and from today's consciousness of wide layers of the working class and unalterably leading to one final conclusion; the conquest of power by the proletariat.[40]

But because Trotsky decided to proclaim the International without having a base in the working class, he was impelled to draw up these 'transitional demands' and formulate them in a fixed system, in isolation from and in advance of mass struggles. This was a false method. Demands which really stem from 'today's consciousness' and actually lead to the 'conquest of power' cannot simply be drawn out of the head of a theoretician, no matter how brilliant, but must be the articulation of the struggles of the masses. For this there is required a party with roots to act as a two way transmission between the workers and the leadership. The Fourth International, however, was too weak to play this role. Trotsky's 'transitional programme', *The Death Agony of Capitalism and the Tasks of the Fourth International*, was accepted without amendment and almost without discussion, but its demands—for a sliding scale of wages, for the opening of the books of big business, for the nationalisation of the banks, for the workers' militia—were never taken up by the workers.

Nor is it possible, as Trotsky assumed, to predict accurately and draw up in advance the programme of the revolution. The overall lines of battle can be foreseen, but not the particular forms of the struggle, and yet it is on these particular forms that specific demands must be based. To lead the Russian Revolution the Bolsheviks had to completely revise their programme, and even such basic slogans as 'Down with the Provisional Government' and 'All Power to the Soviets' had at times to be withdrawn and then advanced again.

The second problem would have been that Trotsky's perspective included a 'new and grand regrouping of the workers' ranks'. This would have been bound to occur through splits in the social-democratic and Stalinist parties and through the emergence of many new revolutionary and semi-revolutionary organisations. Yet Trotsky, by founding the International before any of these developments had taken place or even begun, was attempting to prejudge quite specifically the organisational form taken by this regroupment. In such circumstances the prior existence of an International of sects, with many sectarian habits, which these new organisations and movements would have been required to join, would most likely have constituted a serious obstacle to the creation of a genuine mass workers' International.

In reviewing the question of the Fourth International and Trotsky's theory of the party, it is useful to refer to words he wrote in 1928 (directed against the Stalinist policy of the Anglo-Russian Trade Union Committee):

> It is the worst and most dangerous thing if a manoeuvre arise out of the impatient opportunistic endeavour to outstrip the development of one's own party and to leap over the necessary stages of its development (it is precisely here that no stages must be leaped over).[41]

The proclamation of the International may not have been opportunism, but it was certainly an attempt to outstrip the development of his own party. Essentially it was a grand gesture, the raising aloft of a spotless revolutionary banner. As such it played its part, along with the rest of Trotsky's work, in keeping alive the flame of unfalsified marxism when it was all but extinguished, but it also bequeathed to the Trotskyist movement a false view of the role and nature of revolutionary leadership, a number of misconceptions about 'the programme' and 'transitional demands' and a host of illusions as to its own strength and significance.

3. The degeneration of the Fourth International

At this point it is important to look briefly at what happened to the Fourth International after Trotsky's death, for it was then that the mistakes of Trotsky's last years fully revealed themselves. In 1938 Trotsky had written:

> If our International be still weak in numbers, it is strong in doctrine, programme, tradition, in the incomparable tempering of its cadres. Who does not perceive this today, let him in the meantime stand aside. Tomorrow it will become more evident.[42]

The rest of the 'International leadership', without serious experience in the labour movement and without any independent theoretical achievements to their credit, proved incapable of orienting themselves in a changing world.

It is one of the defects of an International without a base that its 'world' perspectives can depart ever further from reality without being subject to the test and check of practice, and this was exactly what happened. Despite all evidence to the contrary, the leadership of the Fourth International clung to its programme and announced the confirmation of its perspectives. At times this process became farcical, as when James P. Cannon, leader of the American Socialist Workers' Party, wrote, six months after VE day:

> Trotsky predicted that the fate of the Soviet Union would be decided in the war. That remains our firm conviction. Only we disagree with some people who carelessly think the war is over . . . The war is not over, and the revolution which we said would issue from the war in Europe is not taken off the agenda.[43]

On other occasions the blindness was more serious, as when Ernest Mandel wrote in 1946:

> There is no reason whatever to assume that we are facing a new epoch of capitalist stabilisation and development. On the contrary, the war has acted only to aggravate the disproportion between the increased productivity of the capitalist economy and the capacity of the world market to absorb it.[44]

In such a situation splits and splintering of the movement were inevitable. The issue which produced these splits and wrecked the International was the 'Russian question' and, deriving from it, the question of Eastern Europe. For Trotsky, Russia remained a workers' state because of its nationalised property relations, but the role of the Stalinist bureaucracy was seen as reactionary at home and counter-revolutionary in the world arena. This last assumption was in fact the historical justification for the existence of the Fourth International. The communist conquest of Eastern Europe was completely excluded in this analysis, but once it occurred, another question arose which could not be avoided and could not be answered by reference to 'the programme': what was the class character of the East European communist states? Here the

Trotskyist movement was caught on the horns of a dilemma. If the East European countries were workers' states, then not only did this make nonsense of the view that Stalinism was counter-revolutionary, but also it contradicted the marxist theory of socialist revolution, for in almost all cases the working classes of Eastern Europe had played no part in their 'emancipation'. If they remained capitalist, then how could the complete identity of their economic, social and political structure with that of the Soviet Union be explained? The only way out consistent with revolutionary marxism was to abandon the characterisation of Russia as a workers' state,[45] but this would have meant explicit revision of the sacred programme.

Instead the Fourth International zig-zagged and split. At first it tried to maintain the position of the 'buffer-states' being still capitalist, then under the impact of the 1948 Stalin-Tito split, it went over to the implicitly pro-Stalinist view that the Red Army had given birth to a string of 'deformed workers' states'. This was accompanied by an opportunistic attempt to flirt with Marshal Tito, and then, under the leadership of Michel Pablo, a massive lurch towards Stalinism which culminated in the theory that a new world war was approaching in which the Stalinist parties would be forced to radicalise themselves. From this Pablo drew the logical conclusion that the Trotskyist parties should dissolve themselves and resume the position of a left tendency within the communist parties. This whole process had been accompanied by innumerable splits and expulsions, but now a major break occurred. Large sections of the International, led by the American SWP, recoiled at this liquidationism and broke with the leadership—but it was merely Pablo's conclusions that were rejected, not his premises. The International movement founded by Trotsky was now in ruins—theoretically, politically and organisationally.

The upshot of this whole sorry tale is that today there are at least four organisations claiming to be *the* Fourth International and numerous others trying to reconstruct it. In Britain alone there are now something in the region of a dozen 'orthodox' Trotskyist groups all of whom claim adherence to the 'gospel' of the 1938 programme.

Naturally the Leninist theory of the party, for so long defended by Trotsky, has not remained unscathed by this degeneration of Trotskyism. While all Trotskyist sects adhere to the letter of this theory, its 'spirit' has undergone two kinds of revision. The first could be characterised as extreme dogmatic sectarianism. In this variant the organisation, no matter how manifest its smallness and insignificance, proclaims and demands its right to the leadership of the working class. It defines itself as the revolutionary party not on the basis of its role in the class struggle but on the basis of its possession of the 'correct theory' and the 'correct line'. Essentially the party is seen as separate, not only from the working class as a whole but also from the advanced workers. If, for Lenin, the party was both educator and educated, in this version of Trotskyism the party attempts to play schoolmaster to the working class. Internally such organisations tend to authoritarianism and witch-hunting and even at times to the cult of the leader. Externally they exhibit gross delusions of grandeur, paranoia and above all an inability to look reality in the face.

The second variation can be described as petty-bourgeois opportunism. Although ritual obeisance is paid on occasion to 'the role of the working class', the failure to achieve a base in the working class is, in practice, accepted as a fact of life and substitutes are sought. These substitutes range from movements in solidarity with the third world, to students in revolt, to black power, to women's liberation, but all of them involve, a) remaining within and adapting to a petty-bourgeois milieu, and b) postponing to the indefinite future the central task of penetrating and organising the industrial working class. The sect thus comes to resemble an academic discussion group, with a premium on theoretical sophistication, which is absolutely uninhabitable for workers.

Both these versions of 'Trotskyism' rely heavily for their theory of the party on the theory of the early Lenin that socialism must be introduced into the working class from the outside, for both of them use it as an alibi and justification for their isolation from the working class. In fact, in the name of Lenin and Trotsky, they have arrived at a complete caricature of the authentic Leninist and Trotskyist theory of the party.

Of course it is unreasonable to hold Trotsky responsible for all the absurdities committed by his epigones. Nonetheless there is a certain continuity between the errors in his conception of the Fourth International and its later evolution. To employ a metaphor of Trotsky's, the scratch in his theory of the party, produced by the desperate circumstances of the 1930s, became infected and led ultimately to the gangrene of abandoning the conception of the revolutionary party as the organisation of the advanced workers.

6.

Gramsci's Modern Prince

While a beleaguered Trotsky fought to preserve and apply the Leninist theory of the party, another marxist, Antonio Gramsci, worked for 11 years in a fascist prison to develop new and original ideas on revolutionary strategy. The fruit of this immense labour, and the centrepiece of Gramscian strategy, was a new conception of the role and tasks of the revolutionary party, which constitutes the only fundamental addition to the marxist theory of the party since Lenin. Gramsci was able to achieve this breakthrough above all because of the unique philosophical perspective from which he approached the problem of the party. Consequently any analysis of Gramsci's theory of the party must begin with a consideration of the philosophical premises on which it was based.

1. The philosophy of praxis

Like Georg Lukacs, the other outstanding marxist philosopher of the inter-war period, Gramsci came to marxism through Hegel and so 'through philosophy'. The key figures in Gramsci's intellectual formation were Benedetto Croce and Antonio Labriola. Croce was an idealist philosopher for whom the central purpose of philosophy was the understanding of history and who therefore called himself an 'absolute historicist'. Gramsci regarded him as the highest representative of Italian bourgeois culture and indeed as one of the premier spokesmen of liberalism in the world. Croce was a critic of marxism but for Gramsci his work was on a much more advanced intellectual level than that of the vulgar marxism and positivism prevalent in pre-1914 Italy. Thus Gramsci's relationship with Croce parallels that between Marx and Hegel—at first under his influence, then more and more seeing him as a major figure who has to be challenged and superceded in a new synthesis. What Gramsci took from Croce and developed was the rejection of economic determinism and positivism and the importance of the 'ethico-political' or 'ideological' moment in history.

The bridge between marxism and Crocean idealism was provided by Antonio Labriola, the 'founding father' of Italian marxism at the end of the nineteenth century. Labriola was a professor of philosophy at the University of Rome who came to marxism late in life having been a leading figure in the Italian hegelian school. It was Labriola who first introduced the term 'the philosophy of praxis', used by Gramsci as a substitute for 'marxism' in the *Prison Notebooks* in order to get past the prison censor.[1] Gramsci had a high regard for Labriola, valuing especially his emphasis on the unity of theory and practice and the independence of marxism from any other philosophical currents. In the *Prison Notebooks* Gramsci describes him as 'the only man who has attempted to build up the philosophy of praxis scientifically'.[2]

The direction in which Gramsci's ideas were moving was clearly shown by the article with which he greeted the Russian Revolution, *The Revolution against Das Kapital*, in which he praised the Bolsheviks for their refusal to be bound by iron historical laws. And when, after the first world war, Gramsci became a fully-fledged marxist and communist, his version of marxism was completely different from the orthodox 'scientific' materialism which characterised the Second International, and which largely dominated the Third International as well, except for Lenin who had revised his philosophical position in 1914.

For the mature Gramsci of the *Prison Notebooks* 'the philosophy of praxis is absolute "historicism", the absolute secularisation and earthliness of thought, an absolute humanism of history'.[3] It is totally opposed to all forms of transcendentalism, be it the transcendentalism of an abstract 'human nature' or 'man in general', of religion and derivative idealist philosophies, or the transcendentalism of metaphysical materialism basing itself on 'objective laws'.

By defining marxism in an historicist/humanist way, Gramsci separates himself not only from Bukharin and Kautsky and from the neo-Kantians but also from Plekhanov, the philosophical teacher of all the Russian marxists, and this leads him to a critique of the standard presentation of issues which are of the greatest importance for the theory of the party: fatalism, prediction and economic determinism.

As we have frequently pointed out, fatalistic interpretations of marxism have repeatedly hindered understanding of the role of the party, and it is one of Lenin's great achievements that he broke with the Second International's fatalist conception of organisation. But what distinguishes Gramsci from Lenin, Trotsky and other opponents of fatalism is that the latter never really confronted fatalism as such at a philosophical level. The basic argument was always avoided by introducing the time factor. Of course *in the long run*, they would say, the unity of the proletariat, the victory of socialism etc. is inevitable, but the question is how to speed up this process, what *we* should do *now* and so on. In this way the baleful effects of fatalism were repeatedly warded off, but because of the concession of *ultimate* inevitability, fatalism itself was never fundamentally refuted. For Gramsci, however, although he recognises the historically 'useful' role played by fatalism, there is no such basic equivocation. 'It should be noted how the deterministic, fatalistic, and mechanistic element has been a direct ideological "aroma" emanating from the philosophy of praxis, rather like religion or drugs (in their stupefying effect).'[4]

In periods of defeat the fatalist view that 'history is on our side' has been a great source of strength and resistance, but when the proletariat takes the stage as the active director of events (i.e. in a revolution) 'mechanicism at a certain point becomes an imminent danger'.[5]

For the deterministic marxist the great strength of marxism as against bourgeois ideology is its ability to foresee the future because of its insight into the 'laws of history'. This claim is made by Bukharin, and it is a recurring theme in the writings of Trotsky and many others. Gramsci, however, writes that:

> In reality one can 'scientifically' foresee only the struggle, but not the concrete moments of the struggle, which cannot but be the results of opposing forces in continuous movement, which are never reducible to fixed quantities since within them quantity is continually becoming quality. In reality one can 'foresee' to the extent that one acts, to the extent that one applies a voluntary effort and therefore contributes concretely to creating the result 'foreseen'. Prediction reveals itself not as a scientific act of knowledge, but as the abstract expression of the effort made, the practical way of creating a collective will.[6]

If, for Gramsci, fatalism was akin to religion, then economic determinism was little better than superstition and a complete vulgarisation of marxism. Against economic determinism as a historical methodology he cites 'the authentic testimony of Marx, the author of concrete political and historical works'.[7]

Gramsci sees 'economism' or syndicalism as a tendency in the working-class movement as derived more from laissez-faire liberalism[8] (the free play of economic forces) than from marxism, which aims through politics at the subordination of economic forces to man's will. Syndicalism is the theory of an oppressed class 'which is prevented by this theory from ever becoming dominant'.[9]

Ultra-left electoral abstentionism, absolute rejection of 'compromises' and hostility to alliances are all linked by Gramsci with 'economism' in that they are all based on the conviction that economic laws (especially as manifested in capitalist crises) will of themselves lead to socialism. To Gramsci this view of the role of economic crises was 'out and out historical mysticism, the awaiting of a sort of miraculous illumination'.[10] On the contrary:

> it may be ruled out that immediate economic crises of themselves produce fundamental historical events: they can simply create a terrain more favourable to the dissemination of certain modes of thought, and certain ways of posing and resolving questions involving the entire subsequent development of national life.[11]

For Gramsci a genuine marxist analysis of a situation must be a concrete study of the relation of forces in the situation with a view to changing it. Such an analysis must incorporate and distinguish at least three 'moments' or 'levels'.[12]

1. 'The relation of social forces closely linked to the structure, objective, independent of human will and which can be measured with the systems of the exact or physical sciences'. On this basis one can discover 'whether in a particular society there exist the necessary and sufficient conditions for its transformation'.

2. The relation of political forces: 'an evaluation of the homogeneity, self awareness and organisation attained by the various social classes'.

3. The relation of military forces. 'Historical development oscillates continually between the first and the third moment with the mediation

of the second',[13] writes Gramsci, and it is precisely with the second, mediating, moment of politics that he is particularly concerned.

Gramsci, then, assigns to philosophies, conceptions of the world and the ideas men hold an important and active role in the making of history. Naturally this opens him to charges of voluntarism and idealism (and such charges were frequently forthcoming in inner-party struggles). In fact Gramsci is concerned not with philosophy in the abstract, but with the concrete historical development of particular philosophies, and above all with their impact on the everyday thinking and 'common sense' of the masses.

> For a mass of people to be led to think coherently in the same coherent fashion about the present world is a 'philosophical' event far more impor-tant and 'original' than the discovery by some philosophical 'genius' of a truth which remains the property of small groups of intellectuals.[14]

Gramsci insists that 'everyone is a philosopher, though in his own way and unconsciously',[15] but what is necessary is to transform that which is implicit, contradictory and fragmented in the masses into a critical and systematic awareness which can result in the formation of a popular col-lective will to action. But a world outlook does not grow spontaneously in isolated individuals. The formation of a collective will requires a point of origin and a point of dissemination. There must be an active force working to develop it in both theory and practice.[16]

Thus Gramsci's philosophy of praxis with its emphasis on conscious human agency in history and its rejection of all mechanical or rigid determinism led directly to the question of the revolutionary party and made him superbly equipped to deal with it. But on the basis of philo-sophical sophistication alone, Gramsci would not have been able to sig-nificantly advance the theory of the party.[17] For Gramsci's theory of the party, there was a second precondition: profound involvement in politi-cal practice in the working-class movement and the concrete analysis thereof. It is to this that we now turn.

2. The Italian experience—revolution and defeat

The decisive political experience for the shaping of Gramsci's thought was the rising of the Italian workers, spearheaded by the proletariat of Turin in 1919 and 1920. Gramsci's intervention in these events, through the weekly journal *L'Ordine Nuovo*, brought him into the closest contact with the Turin workers. He recalled that

> At that time no initiative was taken that was not tested in reality . . . if the opinions of the workers were not taken fully into account. For this reason, our initiatives appeared as the interpretation of a felt need, never as the cold application of intellectual schema.[18]

Gramsci's great achievement in *L'Ordine Nuovo* was the translation into Italy of the Russian idea of soviets, through the development of the already existing factory internal commissions into factory councils as the foundation of a new state. In an important passage written in 1920 Gramsci summed up his basic conception of communism.

> We have therefore maintained: 1. that the revolution is not necessarily proletarian and communist if it proposes and obtains the overthrow of the bourgeois state; 2. nor is it proletarian and communist if it proposes and obtains the destruction of the representative institutions and administrative machine through which the central government exercises the political power of the bourgeoisie; 3. it is not proletarian and communist even if the wave of popular insurrection places power in the hands of men who call themselves (and sincerely are) communists. The revolution is proletarian and communist only insofar as it liberates proletarian and communist forces of production, forces that have been developing within the society ruled by the capital class. It is proletarian and communist insofar as it advances and promotes the growth and systematisation of proletarian and communist forces that can begin the patient, methodical work necessary for the construction of a new order in the relations of production and distribution.[19]

This emphasis on the creative, constructive aspect of the workers' revolution as against the destructive aspect of overthrowing capitalism was to remain a constant theme in Gramsci's thought.

But this experience was also a negative one in that it revealed the decisive weakness of the Italian Socialist Party (PSI) and the whole tradition of Italian maximalist socialism. The mainstream of Italian socialism completely failed to appreciate the significance of the factory councils, regarding them as a threat to the established order of the trade unions, and the Turin proletariat was left to fight alone. At the crucial moment, the PSI remained bureaucratically paralysed and unable or unwilling to give coherent leadership to the rising revolutionary movement; as a result the initiative was lost and the way opened for the vicious counter-revolution which had its climax in Mussolini's march on Rome. Gramsci's response to this betrayal was a devastating critique entitled *Toward a Renewal of the Socialist Party*[20] in which he indicted the party leadership for its failure to create a homogenous fighting party purged of its reformist and non-communist elements, its failure to involve the party in the life of the Third International, its lack of a revolutionary opposition in the General Confederation of Labour, its attachment to parliamentary democracy and its abstentionist refusal to launch a struggle for power. These theses, which received the endorsement of Lenin, concluded that,

> the existence of a cohesive and highly disciplined communist party with factory, trade-union and co-operative cells, that can co-ordinate and centralise in its central executive committee the whole revolutionary action of the proletariat, is the fundamental and indispensable condition for any experiment in soviets.[21]

Thus not only Gramsci's philosophical position but also his practical experience led him to the question of the party. At first, however, his originality was masked and he was unable to pursue an independent policy. This was due partly to the pressure of day-to-day events in the period of growing fascist repression, and partly to the position in which he found himself within the newly formed Communist Party of Italy (PCI). The PCI was split between the dominating figure of Amadeo Bordiga, an unbending ultra-leftist, and an opportunist right wing led by Angelo Tasca. Gramsci disagreed profoundly with Bordiga, but valued his presence in the party leadership and was unwilling to challenge him for fear of handing the party over to Tasca. It was not until his incarceration in 1926 that Gramsci had the opportunity to develop and expound his ideas, and by this time events on the world scene also loomed large in his concerns. He wished to learn the lessons of the defeat of the post-war revolutionary wave, not just in Italy, but throughout Europe; and in the growth of the fascist corporate state and the emergence of Fordism in America, Gramsci discerned new developments in capitalism which would pose new strategic problems for the workers' movement.

This was the background against which Gramsci, in his prison writings, began to elaborate his concept of the revolutionary party.

3. The 'Modern Prince' and the dual perspective

In the *Prison Notebooks* Gramsci approaches the question of the party through a study of Machiavelli's *The Prince*. The significance of Machiavelli for Gramsci is that he represented a pioneering attempt in Italy to show how to create a national collective will for the foundation of a new state (a unified bourgeois Italy). Machiavelli was a 'precocious Jacobin',[22] who through the myth-figure of 'the Prince' set out the political leadership, the strategy and the tactics necessary for the achievement of this end. The foundation of a new *workers'* state also requires such political leadership—a 'modern prince'. But Gramsci argues:

> The modern prince . . . cannot be a real person, a concrete individual. It can only be an organism, a complex element of society in which a collective will which has already been recognised and has to some extent asserted itself in action, begins to take concrete form. History has already provided this organism, and it is the political party—the first cell in which there come together germs of a collective will tending to become universal and total.[23]

Just as Machiavelli shows the necessary characteristics of a successful prince, so Gramsci proceeds, basing himself throughout on the philosophical position we have outlined above, to discuss the necessary characteristics of the revolutionary party. Unfortunately this is not done systematically, but in a series of very rich and complicated observations which are more or less disconnected and in which prescriptions for the marxist party intermingle with analytical points about parties in general. Thus any relatively brief exposition of these ideas, such as this study, must necessarily attempt to pick out the main themes and give them a structure not present (at least explicitly) in the original. This must to some extent be an arbitrary and unsatisfactory process, but it is unavoidable.

A useful starting point for understanding the originality of Gramsci's theory is his notion of the 'dual perspective' with which the party must operate. The term itself actually derives from Section XIII of the *Theses on Tactics* adopted under the inspiration of Zinoviev by the Fifth World Congress of the Comintern;[24] but it is clear that Gramsci invests the concept with much greater universal significance and deeper content than its originator intended. He writes:

The dual perspective can present itself on various levels, from the most elementary to the most complex: but these can all theoretically be reduced to two fundamental levels, corresponding to the dual nature of Machiavelli's Centaur—half-animal and half-human. They are the levels of force and consent, authority and hegemony, violence and civilisation, of the individual moment and the universal moment ('church' and 'state') of agitation and propaganda, of tactics and of strategy etc.[25]

Gramsci resists any mechanical separation of the two levels or any attempt to present them as successive stages, separate in time. The element of consent is always present in the application of force, and the element of force is always present in the achievement of consent. The editors of the English edition of *Selections from the Prison Notebooks* comment:

> Perhaps one can see here an attempt to theorise the struggle Gramsci had conducted in the PCI against Bordiga on the one hand and Tasca on the other. Bordiga in this schema would represent an undialectical isolation of the moment of force, domination etc., Tasca a parallel isolation of the moment of consent, hegemony; Gramsci sought to theorise the unity of the two perspectives.[26]

But it is also true that, just as in the revolutionary dialectic of destruction/reconstruction Gramsci emphasises reconstruction, so, while never losing sight of the moment of force, it is the moment of consent which Gramsci emphasises and on which he develops his researches. The reason for this stress is partially polemical (i.e. the struggle against Bordigism) but primarily Gramsci's profound reappraisal of the tasks facing revolutionary parties as a result of the defeat of the post-war revolutionary wave and the development of modern capitalism.

If the revolutionary party must pursue a 'dual perspective', it is because the ruling class maintains itself by the same method—by a combination of dictatorship and hegemony, which are respectively institutionalised in political state power and in civil society. But repressive state power and the institutions of civil society do not develop evenly or stand in the same relationship to each other at all times or in all countries. The revolutionary party must make a concrete analysis of this relationship and shape its strategy accordingly. In particular Gramsci believed that the post-war failure of the revolution in the West was the consequence of a basic difference between Russia and the West in this respect.

> In Russia the state was everything, civil society was primordial and gelat-
> inous; in the West, there was a proper relation between state and civil
> society and when the state trembled a sturdy structure of civil society was
> at once revealed.[27]

And also

> in the case of the most advanced states . . . 'civil society' has become a
> very complex structure and one which is resistant to the catastrophic
> 'incursions' of the immediate economic element (crises, depressions,
> etc.)[28]

In Russia therefore the capitalist state stood isolated in its repressive
functions and was susceptible to a speedy frontal attack, but in the
West where capitalism was older and had struck much deeper roots
in society a different strategy was required. Gramsci, using an analogy
from military strategy, terms this 'the war of position', as against the
previous 'war of manoeuvre'.[29] At other points in the *Notebooks* Gramsci
poses the question of transition from war of manoeuvre to war of
position differently—not in terms of Russia and the West, but in terms
of time scale. 'In the present epoch the war of movement took place
politically from March 1917 to March 1921; this was followed by a war
of position.'[30]

There need be no contradiction here, as Gramsci may be suggesting
that the war of manoeuvre was always inadequate for advanced capitalism, but that it was only after the defeats of 1921 that this began to be
realised (with the turn to the united-front policy by the Comintern).

In contrast to the war of manoeuvre which offers the prospect of
quick victory, the war of position implies a long drawn out 'reciprocal siege'[31] which demands an 'unprecedented concentration of hegemony'.[32] The struggle of the revolutionary party to undermine the consent
given by the masses to the authority of the ruling class (which is secured
through a thousand institutional and associational channels and pen-
etrates deeply into everyday 'common sense' thought) and to establish
its own hegemony must take place on three related levels. The first is the
question of alliances:

> The proletariat can become the leading and ruling class to the extent to
> which it succeeds in creating a system of class alliances which enables it

to mobilise the majority of the working population against capitalism and the bourgeois state.[33]

Such alliances, Gramsci points out, must inevitably contain an element of compromise. 'If the union of two forces is necessary in order to defeat a third . . . the only concrete possibility is compromise.'[34] The aversion on principle of ultra-lefts to compromises and therefore to alliances is, he argues, a product of their fatalistic 'economism':

> since favourable conditions are inevitably going to appear . . . it is evident that any deliberate initiative tending to predispose and plan these conditions is not only useless but even harmful.[35]

Gramsci, on the contrary, placed especial importance on the strategy of alliances, because in Italy the revolution could be made only through an alliance of the northern proletariat and the southern peasantry—a question on which the record of Italian socialism was poor. The overcoming of all sectarian tendencies in the party is a precondition of its achieving hegemony. Thus it is not surprising that Gramsci was completely opposed to the tactics of the Stalinist 'third period', although this was concealed at the time.[36]

The second level of the struggle for hegemony is that of the education of one's own forces. For the war of position it is not possible to rely solely on the mobilisation of the mass of workers behind immediate demands and slogans. Rather they have to be won over at the basic level of their world view and welded into a 'permanently organised and long prepared force which can be put into the field at the favourable moment'.[37] To do this the party must

> never tire of repeating its own arguments (though offering literary vari- ation of form): repetition is the best didactic means for working on the popular mentality (and must) work incessantly to raise the intellectual level of ever-growing strata of the populace.[38]

This requires a correction of the balance between agitation and propaganda (in favour of propaganda),[39] for the party must not only be an expression of the class but must 'react energetically [upon it] in order to develop, solidify and universalise [it]'.[40] Sectarian dogmatism in theory is fatal for such a work of 'intellectual and moral reform', and Gramsci was always opposed to the appearance of, for example, crude anti-clericalism in socialist propaganda. The raising of the intellectual level of the masses cannot be brought about by the imposition of dogma, but must come through separating the element of 'good sense' in their 'common sense' from the element of confused prejudice and through working to expand and develop it. This requires a sophisticated and non-economistic marxist method.

The third level, which conditions the success of the first two, might be termed the struggle for the intellectuals, and this in turn has two aspects. First, it is necessary to create a stratum of intellectuals 'organic' to the working class. Here Gramsci is not using intellectual in the usual way to signify the man of letters, the philosopher, the abstract thinker etc, but to refer to the worker who has a clear conception of the world and of his aims, is an active participant in practical life, a 'permanent persuader' and who constitutes the organising directive element in the working class. In other words, the proletarian counterpart to the organic intellectuals of the bourgeoisie—the industrial technicians, the political economists, the judges and lawyers etc.[41]

The formation of 'elites of intellectuals of a new type which arise directly out of the masses, but remain in contact with them to become, as it were, the whalebone in the corset . . . is what really modifies the "ideological panorama" of the age'.[42]

But Gramsci is not utopian about this. He is fully aware from his own experience of the difficulty of intellectual labour and systematic study, especially for the worker, and recognises that the formation of worker-intellectuals is a long slow process that can be completed only after the conquest of state power.

It is also necessary, however, to carry out work in relation to non-proletarian intellectuals, though again Gramsci is clear about the limitations of this.

> The intellectuals develop slowly, much more slowly than any other social group, because of their own nature and historical role . . . To think it possible that this type can, as a mass, break with the whole of the past in order to place itself wholeheartedly on the side of a new ideology, is absurd. It is absurd for the intellectuals as a mass, and perhaps absurd also for very many intellectuals taken individually, despite all the honest efforts they make and want to make. Now the intellectuals interest us as a mass, and not only as individuals. It is certainly important and useful for the proletariat that one or more intellectuals, individually, adhere to its

programme and its doctrine, merge themselves with the proletariat, and become and feel themselves an integral part of it . . . But it is also important and useful that a break of an organic kind, characterised historically, is caused inside the mass of intellectuals: that there is formed, as a mass formation, a left-wing tendency, in the modern sense of the word, that is, one which is orientated towards the revolutionary proletariat.[43]

This is necessary not only because it undermines the exercise of bourgeois hegemony in general, but because Gramsci considers that the intellectuals play a key role in maintaining the system of alliances constructed by the ruling class with subordinate strata, and therefore can play a corresponding role in the system of alliances that must be constructed by the party of the proletariat. With regard to Italy, Gramsci analyses the role of intellectuals in the southern agrarian bloc, where they acted as mediators between the peasants and the big landowners; and argues that a left tendency among the intellectuals is one of the prerequisites for breaking this bloc and securing the alliance of the peasantry with the proletariat. In this connection Gramsci notes that the more developed the stratum of organic intellectuals of the proletariat, the greater the pole of attraction the revolutionary party will constitute for the intellectuals in general, and that such intellectuals are likely to be repelled if presented with a vulgar materialist version of marxist theory.

4. Spontaneity and leadership

Underlying the whole of Gramsci's theory of the party is his conception of the relationship of spontaneity and conscious leadership, which can be regarded, at least partially, as equivalent to the relationship between party and class and which is the fundamental question of the marxist theory of the party. His presentation of the problem is a clear advance on that which was achieved by Rosa Luxemburg, the early Lenin or by Lukacs, and corresponds most closely to the position of the mature Lenin. Gramsci begins with a critique of the very concept of pure spontaneity.

It must be stressed that 'pure' spontaneity does not exist in history: it would come to the same thing as 'pure' mechanicity. In the 'most spontaneous' movement it is simply the case that the elements of 'conscious leadership' cannot be checked, have left no reliable document. It may be said that spontaneity is therefore characteristic of the 'history of the subaltern

classes', and indeed of their most marginal and peripheral elements . . .
Hence in such movements there exist multiple elements of 'conscious
leadership' but no one of them is predominant or transcends the level of a
given social stratum's 'popular science'—its 'common sense' or traditional
conception of the world.[44]

Gramsci rejects those who counterpose this spontaneity to marxism
and who extol it as a political method. This mistake in theory and in
practice is based on a 'vulgar contradiction which betrays its manifest
practical origin—i.e. the immediate desire to replace a given leadership
by a different one'.[45] But he is equally opposed to a disdainful attitude
to mass spontaneity.

> Neglecting, or worse still, despising, so-called 'spontaneous' movements,
> i.e. failing to give them a conscious leadership or to raise them to a higher
> plane by inserting them into politics, may often have extremely serious
> consequences. It is almost always the case that a 'spontaneous' movement
> of the subaltern classes is accompanied by a reactionary movement of the
> right-wing of the dominant class, for concomitant reasons. An economic
> crisis, for instance, engenders on the one hand discontent among the
> subaltern classes and spontaneous mass movements, and on the other
> conspiracies among the reactionary groups, who take advantage of the
> objective weakening of the government in order to attempt coups d'état.
> Among the effective causes of the coups must be included the failure of
> the responsible groups to give any conscious leadership to the spontane-
> ous revolts or to make them into a positive political factor.[46]

Although Gramsci follows this with a reference to the rising of the
Sicilian Vespers of 1282 (probably to divert the censor) he clearly has in
mind the attitude of the PSI and the Bordigists to the events of 1919–20
as a factor in permitting the triumph of Mussolini.

As an example of the correct relationship between spontaneity and
conscious leadership Gramsci cites the work of the Ordine Nuovo group.

> The Turin movement was accused simultaneously of being 'spontaneist' and
> 'voluntarist' or Bergsonian. This contradictory accusation, if one analyses
> it, only testifies to the fact that the leadership given to the movement was
> both creative and correct. This leadership was not 'abstract'; it neither
> consisted in mechanically repeating scientific or theoretical formulae, nor
> did it confuse politics, real action, with theoretical disquisition. It applied
> itself to real men, formed in specific historical relations, with specific

feelings, outlooks, fragmentary conceptions of the world, etc. which were the result of 'spontaneous' combinations of a given situation of material production with the 'fortuitous' agglomeration within it of disparate social elements. The element of 'spontaneity' was not neglected and even less despised. It was *educated*, directed, purged of extraneous contaminations; the aim was to bring it in line with modern theory [marxism]—but in a living and historically effective manner. The leaders themselves spoke of the 'spontaneity' of the movement and rightly so. This assertion was a stimulus, a tonic, an element of unification in depth; above all it denied that the movement was arbitrary, a cooked-up venture, and stressed its historical necessity. It gave the masses a 'theoretical' consciousness of being creators of *historical* and institutional *values*, of being founders of a State. This unity between 'spontaneity' and 'conscious leadership' or 'discipline' is precisely the real political action of the subaltern classes, insofar as this is mass politics and not merely an adventure by groups claiming to represent the masses.[47]

As a result of this analysis Gramsci then raises what he calls a 'fundamental theoretical question' which relates, though from a different angle, to Lenin's view in *What is to be done?* that socialism must be introduced into the working class from the outside. Gramsci asks:

Can modern theory [marxism] be in opposition to the 'spontaneous' feelings of the masses? ('Spontaneous' in the sense that they are not the result of any systematic educational activity on the part of an already conscious leading group, but have been formed through everyday experience illuminated by 'common sense' i.e. by the traditional popular conception of the world.)[48]

Gramsci's answer:

It cannot be in opposition to them. Between the two there is a 'quantitative' difference of degree not one of quality. A reciprocal 'reduction' so to speak, a passage from one to the other and vice versa, must be possible.[49]

The contrast between Gramsci's view and that of both the early Lenin and Lukacs should be clear. Gramsci establishes the link and reciprocal relationship (which is denied in *What is to be done?* and *History and Class Consciousness*) between the actual consciousness, experience and practice of the working class and potential socialist class-consciousness. And he does this without falling into the opposite error of spontaneism.

But Gramsci does not deal only with the strategic tasks of the party and with what its relationship should be to the mass of the class. The *Prison Notebooks* also contain a number of comments on the organisation and internal life necessary for it to be able to play the role assigned to it. Indeed he goes so far as to say that 'the way in which the party functions provides discriminating criteria'[50] for judging the party as a whole. 'When the party is progressive it functions "democratically" (democratic centralism): when the party is regressive it functions "bureaucratically" (bureaucratic centralism).'[51]

At the same time there is no trace of utopianism in Gramsci's picture of the party and its membership. He begins by asserting the 'primordial and (given certain general conditions) [i.e. the existence of class society—J.M.] irreducible fact . . . that there really do exist rulers and ruled, leaders and led',[52] and that although this division has its origin in class divisions, it operates also within socially homogeneous groups and therefore within parties. In line with this premise Gramsci analyses the membership of the party as consisting of three elements:

> 1. A mass element, composed of ordinary, average men, whose participation takes the form of discipline and loyalty, rather than any creative spirit or organisational ability. Without these the party would not exist it is true, but it is also true that neither could it exist with these alone. They are a force insofar as there is somebody to centralise, organise and discipline them . . .
> 2. The principal cohesive element, which centralises nationally and renders effective and powerful a complex of forces which left to themselves would count for nothing. This element is endowed with great cohesive, centralising and disciplinary powers; also—and indeed this is perhaps the basis for the others—with the power of innovation . . .
> 3. An intermediate element, which articulates the first element with the second and maintains contact between them, not only physically but also morally and intellectually.[53]

Nor does Gramsci make any bones about the fact that of the three elements it is the second, the leadership, to which he attaches most importance.

> It is also true that neither could this element form the party alone; however it could do so more than could the first element considered. One

speaks of generals without any army but in reality it is easier to form an army than to form generals.[54]

However this 'realism' is counter-balanced by another equally fundamental premise.

In the formation of leaders . . . is it the intention that there should always be rulers and ruled, or is the objective to create the conditions in which this division is no longer necessary?[55]

Since Gramsci's aim is certainly the latter, the authority of leadership and discipline must not be based on

a passive and supine acceptance of orders, or the mechanical carrying out of an assignment (which, however, will still be necessary on particular occasions) but [on] the conscious and lucid assimilation of the directive to be accomplished.[56]

What must be achieved within the party, therefore, is 'centralism in movement'—i.e. a continual adaptation of the organisation to the real movement, a matching of thrusts from below with orders from above, a continuous insertion of elements thrown up from the depths of the rank-and-file into the solid framework of the leadership apparatus.[57] 'One of the most important questions concerning the political party', Gramsci argues, is 'the party's capacity to react against force of habit.'[58] Parties are created in order to prepare for crisis situations, to be able to act at historical turning points, but often they become routinised and incapable of adapting themselves to new tasks. In this respect the main enemy is bureaucracy.

The bureaucracy is the most dangerously hidebound and conservative force; if it ends up by constituting a compact body, which stands on its own and feels itself independent of the mass of members, the party ends up by becoming anachronistic and at moments of acute crisis it is voided of its social content and left as though suspended in mid-air.[59]

But this question also must not be viewed only from one side—for while there is the problem of habit and routine, there is also the need to maintain continuity and establish a tradition.

> There is a danger of becoming 'bureaucratised' it is true, but every organic
> continuity presents this danger, which must be watched. The danger of
> discontinuity, of improvisation, is still greater.[60]

Thus in the case of the internal life of the party, just as with the 'dual
perspective', and the relationship of the party to the class, Gramsci
envisages a dialectical unity between leaders and led, discipline and
initiative, continuity and change.

5. A provisional assessment

What of the claim that Gramsci is 'the theoretician of revolution in the
west'? Leninism proved itself in Russia and in so doing broke new ground
of universal significance. It was Gramsci, through his analysis of the
development of civil society and the deep roots of bourgeois hegemony,
who saw more clearly than anyone else the basic difference between
Russia and advanced capitalism, and therefore the broadening of the
framework of Leninism that would be necessary. Lenin and Trotsky, as
Gramsci was aware, had by 1921 begun to sense the problem, but Lenin
was preoccupied with Russia and soon to die, and Trotsky, also beset
with other difficulties, was unable to develop his insights beyond the
level of tactics.[61] Gramsci, however, thought through the implications of
his analysis as thoroughly and concretely as the isolation of his prison
cell permitted. Moreover, history has proved to be 'on Gramsci's side' in
this respect. Western capitalism has shown itself to possess far greater
resilience than the theory of the early Comintern marxists allowed for,
and Gramsci's analysis of the expansion of bourgeois social control in his
study of 'Americanism and Fordism' reveals him as a profound prophet of
new tendencies in capitalism.

Philosophically Gramsci has also been justified: by the publication of
Marx's early writings and the *Grundrisse* and by the numerous modern
researches into marxist philosophy. Can any serious marxist today
doubt the baleful influence of fatalism and economic determinism on
the revolutionary movement? Other later marxists approached if not
equalled Gramsci in their insights into the structure of capitalist society
and marxist philosophy, but Gramsci is distinguished from them all in
that he, and he alone, was able to forge these insights into a coherent
revolutionary strategy based on a development of the theory of the party.

Gramsci is thus the only marxist to have added anything fundamentally new to Lenin's theory of the party.

Nevertheless there remains a question mark over Gramsci's contribution. His ideas have never been applied in practice. Like Machiavelli he was not himself in a position to change reality—'only of showing concretely how the historical forces ought to have acted in order to be effective'.[62]

Nor have Gramsci's ideas found other hands to take them up and apply them, and what is more they could not have done so. Gramscian strategy requires as its starting point the existence of a Leninist party, but the combined effects of the long postwar boom and the ravages of Stalinism have meant that such parties have not in fact existed. The basic principles of Bolshevism can, within certain limits (and they are quite narrow limits), guide the activity of a small organisation or even a tiny group. This is not the case with the ideas of Gramsci. The war of manoeuvre, like guerrilla war, can be waged with relatively small forces, but the war of position demands a mass army. Without a mass party alliances will not be alliances between classes in a historical bloc but mere temporary co-operation between groups, which may often serve only to blur theoretical and programmatic differences. Without a mass proletarian base the formation of organic intellectuals and the struggle to win over traditional intellectuals will not, as intended, strengthen proletarian hegemony, but will degenerate into scholastic intellectualism and academicism. Gramsci, it must be remembered, wrote against a background in which the basic ideas of socialism were very widely spread in the working class and the PCI had been founded with a membership of about 40,000, of whom 98 per cent were workers and less than 0.5 per cent (245 in all) intellectuals.[63] To imagine that his ideas can be simply transferred to a situation in which the revolutionary movement is overloaded with students and petty bourgeois and has only the slenderest roots in the working class is crassly ahistorical.

We do not really know what the war of position looks like in its practical details. Thus any judgement of Gramsci's theory of the party must be provisional. If one is impressed and convinced, as it is hard not to be, by the coherence, depth, subtlety and concreteness of Gramsci's ideas, then one must hold that they will face their decisive test in the future when advanced Western capitalism is once again confronted by mass revolutionary workers' parties.

7.

The revolutionary party today

1. The theory of the party since the war

We have now traced the development of the marxist theory of the party from Marx's original establishment of the idea of a party of the working class, through Lenin's concept of the vanguard party, Rosa Luxemburg's emphasis on the creativity of the masses, Trotsky's lonely defence of Leninism, to Gramsci's analysis of the struggle for hegemony. Our account is now essentially complete, for since Trotsky and Gramsci there has been no major contribution to the theory of the party.

The reason for this stagnation is not hard to find. The postwar period has been dominated by the most sustained boom in the history of capitalism, which has resulted for the most part in the reformist integration of the working class. Crushed between the relative passivity of the working class and the dead hand of Stalinist 'orthodoxy', genuine marxism was, as it were, forced underground. Those few who remained committed to the goal of international proletarian revolution were necessarily preoccupied with the defence of marxist fundamentals (the role of the working class, the labour theory of value, the contradictions of capitalism) and with coming to grips with the major changes taking place in the world (the phenomenon of state capitalism, the permanent arms economy, the changes in imperialism). They lacked the practical experience of revolutionary struggle to make the further development of the marxist theory of the party either possible or urgent.

There have been forthcoming, however, a number of non-marxist alternatives to the revolutionary workers' party as means of achieving the overthrow of capitalism. The post-war period has seen the revival of various forms of voluntarism, spontaneism and popular frontism, but all have failed the test of practice. Voluntarism received its most extreme

147

and important expression in the theory that the revolution could be made by a small but determined band of rural guerillas, without waiting for objective conditions to ripen and without mobilising the mass of the working class.[1] But after its initial spectacular success in Cuba,[2] the strategy of the guerilla foco failed to make headway in Latin America and eventually foundered in the Bolivian jungle with the death of Che Guevara in 1967. Nor did the attempt to preserve the method but shift its venue to the towns, exemplified by the Tupamaros of Uruguay, meet with more than temporary success.[3] Spontaneism—the rejection of organisation, authority and above all of the political party—was largely a product of the student revolt which spread across the world in the 1960s. But the highest achievement of this phase of the movement, the French May events of 1968, was also the most compelling demonstration of its inadequacy. Precisely because of the absence of a mass revolutionary workers' party, the French Communist Party was able to dampen down the militancy of the great general strike and engineer a feeble compromise with de Gaulle, thus defusing the acute social crisis almost as rapidly as it had emerged.[4] Finally, the strategy of the popular front and the peaceful transition to socialism were once again put to the test in the shape of the Popular Unity government of Salvador Allende in Chile, with disastrous consequences which are known to all.[5]

This demonstration of the bankruptcy of these alternatives (and the cases just cited are merely the clearest of many examples) has combined with the rapid deepening of the crisis of world capitalism and the consequent rise in working-class struggle during the last decade to refocus attention on the marxist theory of the party. The result has been on the one hand the appearance of a number of studies devoted to disinterring the marxist tradition on the question of the party and indicating perspectives for the present,[6] and on the other the emergence in various countries of sizeable organisations (not mass parties but large enough to constitute a serious beginning) with the aim of building the revolutionary party. It is as a continuation and systematisation of the former project and as an aid to the latter that the present work was conceived. What remains, therefore, is to summarise the main principles of the marxist theory of the party, as drawn from this study of its development, and to indicate key points for their application today.

2. Key characteristics and tasks of the revolutionary party

The role, tasks and organisational forms of the party are not fixed for all time and all places; they must necessarily be derived from and adapted to the concrete situation in which the party operates. Nonetheless, on the basis of over a century and a quarter of struggle, we can make the following generalisations:

The class nature of the party. The revolutionary party must be a *working-class* party. This elementary and fundamental principle, established by Marx, needs repeating once again because it has so often been forgotten or ignored in recent years. The party must be proletarian, not only in the sense that its programme is an articulation of the socialist aspirations of the working class, but also in its social composition and the field of its everyday activities. No guerilla band, peasant movement, student movement or grouping of intellectuals, no matter how fine its programme, can be the substitute for a party with its roots in the industrial proletariat. A young organisation finding itself, as often happens, predominantly petty bourgeois in composition must make a strenuous effort of self-criticism and self-transformation in order to make the transition to a workers' party.

The party as vanguard. The need for a party derives from the uneven development of the working-class, and the party aims to embrace not the entire class (which in 'normal' times is dominated by bourgeois ideology) but its class-conscious vanguard. This point, established by Lenin, has been so often distorted and misinterpreted that it requires the following clarification: the party is a vanguard, but the vanguard is *not* a tiny elite standing outside the main body of the class; it is the hundreds of thousands of workers who actually lead the class in its everyday battles in the factories, the pits, the offices, the housing estates and the streets. The party leads the class, it does not tail-end it, but it leads from within, not from the outside.

The party is an organisation for combat. This has two aspects. Firstly, the party does not claim its leadership of the class as of right but has to fight to win it by producing concrete proposals for action on every issue facing the working class, from the smallest question of factory conditions to the greatest questions of international politics. The party must prove in practice, in struggle, that it is the best defender of the interests of the working class and all the exploited. Secondly, the party must ultimately gear itself for the class struggle in its most acute form, mass uprising and insurrection. This does not mean prematurely adopting a paramilitary stance in such a way as to sacrifice the party's legality and prevent it carrying out its more basic tasks in the everyday struggle, but it does involve, at a certain point, making careful preparations and creating the kind of organisation that can rapidly shift to a military footing. Because in these ways the party is a combat organisation, it has no room for a layer of passive card holders or of privileged, secure bureaucrats. Its membership must be active and self-sacrificial, and is likely therefore to be young.

Democratic centralism. No useful generalisations can be made as to specific organisational structures—these must be extremely flexible—but that the party regime must combine democracy and centralism is not a mere organisational formula, rather it flows directly from the tasks of the party and the nature of the class struggle. Democracy is essential because the party is not the master of the working class but an instrument of its self-emancipation. Without democracy and free discussion there is no way that the party can formulate policies which really meet the needs of the working class and fit the concrete situation. Centralism is essential because the party must wage a bitter struggle against a highly centralised enemy—the capitalist state. Without unity in action, as every trade unionist knows, defeat is inevitable.

With regard to democratic centralism, there are two pitfalls which are particularly likely to afflict new and as yet small organisations of the kind that mostly exist on the revolutionary left round the world today. The first is the danger of a small group, at best the embryo of the party, adopting the full panoply of administrative structures appropriate to a mass party, and so becoming ludicrously top-heavy. The second is the danger, especially when an organisation has to make the transition from propaganda to agitation, of being ultra-democratic and discussing all questions endlessly. The party is not a debating society—it discusses in order to reach a decision, and then carries out that decision in a united fashion.

The independence of the party. The party takes its stand on marxist principle as the representative of the historical interests of the working class—it must never sacrifice its independence to any other political force, openly bourgeois, reformist or centrist. This in no way precludes any number of alliances, compromises, temporary agreements etc. with other organisations, but it does preclude giving up the right to free criticism, a separate political line and a separate organisation. This applies even in the extreme case of entry into or affiliation to a larger party (e.g. the British Labour Party). Dependence, it must be remembered, need not be a matter of formal agreements or limitations. The British Communist Party, for example, is formally an independent organisation, yet politically it is tied to 'left' trade-union leaders and 'left' Labour MPs. A marxist party must never allow itself to become uncritically attached to any populist demagogue or prominent left-reformist, no matter how radical.

The party and the unity of the working class. The party is the vanguard of the class and must maintain its independence, but its aim is the unity of the working class. Three things follow from this. First, that the party must struggle relentlessly as a matter of the strictest principle against all those divisions in the working class—divisions of race, of nationality, between men and women, skilled and unskilled, employed and unemployed, old and young, etc.—which are so assiduously fostered by the ruling class and by means of which it maintains its power. Secondly, the party must not allow its existence as a separate organisation to disrupt the unity needed by the class in its daily struggle against the employers and the state. From this imperative derives the strategy of the united front with reformist organisations, but this strategy (applicable in many but not all conditions) is merely one expression of the general principle governing the party's relationship with all other political tendencies in the working class—march separately, strike together. Thirdly, although the party must guard against the dilution of its programme and policies under pressure from the backward workers, it must on no account fence itself off from these workers and must exploit every avenue to reach them. Thus, while millions of workers remain in reactionary trade unions, the party must work in those unions no matter how treacherous and corrupt their leadership. While the mass of workers retain illusions about social-democratic parties, the party must urge support for those parties against the openly bourgeois parties, so that these illusions can be dispelled by experience. While the majority of the class places its faith in parliamentary democracy, the party must participate in elections, using them to make revolutionary propaganda and to undermine the parliamentary system from within.

The educational tasks of the party. The party must undertake a continuous and complex work of education. It must train revolutionary leaders steeped in the marxist tradition, but capable of making concrete analyses and of independent judgement. It must produce a broad layer of, to use Gramsci's term, 'organic intellectuals', workers with a clear conception of the overall nature of the struggle and the methods of waging it. It must work for the widest possible dissemination of basic marxist and socialist principles amongst the working class by ceaselessly translating its theory into topical and easily understood examples and exposures in its press and all its propaganda. In relation to education, two points have to be borne in mind: the process of education must be predominantly practical rather than academic in character (since the latter leads inevitably to the dominance of petty-bourgeois elements), and, as Rosa Luxemburg emphasised, the party must be able to learn from the workers as well as teach them. The party is the collective memory and brain of the working class, but it is a brain that needs constant renewal and updating.

The struggle for hegemony. The party must work to bring together all the forces of the oppressed in a common struggle against capitalism, under the leadership of the proletariat. Historically and on a world scale this has been principally a question of realising an alliance of the proletariat and the peasantry, and every workers' party must be sure to include in its programme the defence of the interests of the poor peasants. In addition to this, the last decade has seen the emergence of a series of new forces—the black movement, the women's movement and the student movement being the most important—which possess great revolutionary potential but which pose for the party certain strategic problems. On the one hand, and this applies particularly to small organisations without a strong proletarian base, the party can throw itself so uncritically and enthusiastically into these movements that it succumbs to their necessarily fragmented character and neglects its fundamental work in the industrial working class. On the other hand the party can dogmatically dismiss the special problems and claims of the various oppressed strata and present their movements with an ultimatum that they accept in advance the leadership of the proletarian party, which results not in unity but in estrangement. What is needed, therefore, is unconditional support for the justified demands of the oppressed strata combined with principled but patient insistence on the need for unity in the struggle against the common enemy, on the class character of that struggle and on the leading role of the working class. Above all, the full struggle for hegemony, which involves establishing the dominance of revolutionary culture in every area of the social life of the people, can be conducted effectively only by a party which has already secured a substantial base in the working class.

The International. The proletariat is an international class and the socialist revolution is an international process. Consequently all the characteristics of a revolutionary party we have listed here must ultimately be realised on an international scale in a single world party. At the present time such an International does not exist, nor can it be built in a day. A 'world party' consisting, like the Fourth International, of a handful of like-minded sects, is a fiction which cannot produce an international leadership with any real authority. On the other hand, a federation of basically heterogeneous organisations, like the First International, will fall apart at the decisive moment. The Third International was formed on the authority of the victorious Russian Revolution, but a repetition of this sequence of events cannot be passively awaited. How then can the International be built? At present the only realistic course is for the existing revolutionary workers' organisations to engage in practical collaboration wherever possible and in the constant exchange of theoretical positions, so that gradually, on the basis of this joint work and under the impact of events, closer links and greater political homogeneity can be achieved. But this work must be carried out with the clear perspective that its aim is the creation of a new revolutionary workers' International. For the building of revolutionary parties and their international unification is now the principal and most urgent strategic task facing revolutionaries throughout the world. Unless this is achieved, the working class will be unable to resolve in its favour the crisis of capitalism which grows more acute by the day.

Finally, running through everything that the party is and does, the thread connecting all its key characteristics and tasks is the striving to unite theory and practice. The party exists to translate the general aims of socialism into concrete practical activities and to link every immediate struggle to the ultimate aim of socialism. Through the party, theory—the materialist interpretation of history, the analysis of capitalism and its contradictions and the understanding of the historical role of the working class—informs practice, and through the party, practice—the struggle to change the world—stimulates, directs, tests and ultimately realises theory.

When capitalism is stable and the working class presents no open challenge to the system, theory and practice are inevitably divorced. In such conditions the revolutionary party can be prepared but not built. It remains an abstract necessity. But when, as now, the system is racked by crisis, then theory and practice draw together, and building the party becomes no longer an abstract aspiration, but both a practical necessity and a real possibility.

References

1. Karl Marx: Class and party

1. Marx and Engels, *The German Ideology*, cited in R.Dahrendorf, *Class and Class Conflict in Industrial Society*, London 1959, p.14.
2. Marx and Engels, *The Communist Manifesto*, Moscow 1957, p.48.
3. Marx, *Capital*, Vol. III cited in Dahrendorf, *op.cit.* p.13.
4. Marx and Engels, *The Communist Manifesto, op.cit.* p.66.
5. *ibid.* p.58.
6. See Hal Draper, 'The Principle of Self-Emancipation in Marx and Engels', *Socialist Register*, 1972.
7. Marx, *The Eighteenth Brumaire of Louis Bonaparte*, New York 1963, pp.123–24.
8. See Marx, *The Poverty of Philosophy*, Moscow 1966, p.150.
9. Marx and Engels, *The German Ideology*, London 1965, p.78fn.
10. *ibid.* p.61.
11. Marx and Engels, *The Communist Manifesto, op.cit.* p.64.
12. Cited in D.McLellan, *The Thought of Karl Marx*, London 1971, p.177.
13. 'Provisional Rules of the First International', in D.Fernbach (ed.), *Karl Marx: The First International and After*, London 1974, p.82.
14. Marx and Engels, *The Communist Manifesto, op.cit.* p.72.
15. Trotsky was to refer to this passage when arguing his case for a united front against fascism in Germany. See Chapter 5 below.
16. Monty Johnstone, 'Marx and Engels and the Concept of the Party', *Socialist Register*, 1967, p.122.
17. Marx to Freiligrath (1860), cited in D.McLellan, *The Thought of Karl Marx, op.cit.* p.169.
18. Marx and Engels, *Selected Correspondence*, Moscow 1965, p.263.
19. This seems to me to be generally the most desirable procedure, even if it were not, as is the case with Marx, the only possible one.
20. Engels, 'On the History of the Communist League', in Marx and Engels, *Selected Works*, Vol.II, Moscow 1962, p.348.
21. The figure is taken from Monty Johnstone, *op.cit.*

22. Engels, 'Marx and the *Neue Rheinische Zeitung*', in Marx and Engels, *Selected Works*, Vol.II, *op.cit.* p.330.
23. Cited in Franz Mehring, *Karl Marx*, London 1966, p.155.
24. Cited in *ibid.* pp.185–86.
25. Marx, 'The March Address', in Marx and Engels, *Selected Works*, Vol.I, *op.cit.* pp.106–107.
26. *ibid*, p.112.
27. Cited in Franz Mehring, *op.cit.* pp.207–208.
28. Marx to Engels, 11 February 1851, cited in Bertram D. Wolfe, *Marxism: 100 Years in the Life of a Doctrine*, London 1967, p.196.
29. Engels to Marx, 13 February 1851, cited in *ibid.* p.196.
30. Franz Mehring, *op.cit.* p.209.
31. Bertram D. Wolfe, *op.cit.* p.209.
32. Shlomo Avineri, *The Social and Political Thought of Karl Marx*, Cambridge 1969, p.255.
33. Even a cursory glance at the Marx-Engels correspondence reveals that because of their deep bond of friendship and understanding they use all sorts of rash and outrageous expressions which they would have never dreamt of uttering in public statements.
34. Marx to Engels, 25 November 1857, in Marx and Engels, *Selected Correspondence, op.cit.* p.99.
35. Cited in Bertram D. Wolfe, *op.cit.* p.200.
36. Marx to Engels, 4 November 1864, in Marx and Engels, *Selected Correspondence, op.cit.* p.146.
37. It was in answer to Citizen Weston that Marx wrote his famous pamphlet *Wages, Prices and Profit.*
38. See Boris I. Nicolaevsky, 'Secret Societies and the First International', in Milorad Drachovitch (ed.), *The Revolutionary Internationals 1863–1943*, London 1966.
39. Marx to Engels, 4 November 1864, in Marx and Engels, *Selected Correspondence, op.cit.* p.148.
40. *ibid.* p.149.
41. See Hal Draper, *op.cit.*
42. 'Provisional Rules of the First International', in D.Fernbach (ed.), *Karl Marx: The First International and After, op.cit.* p.82.
43. Cited in *ibid.* p.269.
44. *ibid.*
45. Marx and Engels, *Selected Works*, Vol.I, *op.cit.* p.388.
46. Cited in Monty Johnstone, *op.cit.* p.131.
47. Marx, Engels, Lenin, *Anarchism and Anarcho-Syndicalism*, Moscow 1972, p.56.
48. Bakunin to Richard, 1 April 1870, cited in Monty Johnstone, *op.cit.* p.134.
49. Monty Johnstone, *op.cit.* p.134.
50. Marx obtained Bakunin's expulsion, not on a political basis, but by implicating him in the activities of the deluded Russian conspirator, Nechayev, and

by charging him with swindling Marx in connection with 300 roubles for the translation of *Capital.*

51. Cited in D.McLellan, *op.cit.* pp.175–76.
52. Marx to Bolte, 23 November 1871, in Marx and Engels, *Selected Correspondence, op.cit.* pp.270–71.
53. Engels to Bloch, 21–22 September 1890, in Marx and Engels, *Selected Correspondence, op.cit.* p.418.
54. Engels to Bernstein, 27 February–1 March 1883, in Marx and Engels, *Selected Correspondence, op.cit.* p.358.
55. Engels to Bebel, 21 June 1873, *ibid.* pp.283–85.
56. Engels to Sorge, 12–17 September, *ibid.* p.289.
57. Engels, 'Trades Unions II', *The Labour Standard,* 4 June 1881, in W.O.Henderson (ed.), *Engels' Selected Writings,* London 1967, p.109.
58. Engels to F.K.Wischnewstzky, 28 December 1886, in Marx and Engels, *Selected Correspondence, op.cit.* pp.398–99.
59. Engels to Bernstein, 20 October 1882, *ibid.* p.352.
60. *ibid.* p.353.
61. Engels to Bebel, 12 October 1875, *ibid.* p.298.
62. 'Critique of the Gotha Programme', in D.Fernbach (ed.), *Karl Marx: The First International and After, op.cit.*
63. *ibid.* p.355.
64. Marx and Engels to Bebel, Liebknecht, Bracke and others, 17–18 September 1879, in Marx and Engels, *Selected Correspondence, op.cit.* p.327.
65. Engels to Bekker, 1 July 1879, *ibid.* p.328.
66. Marx to Sorge, 19 September 1879, *ibid.* p.328.
67. Marx and Engels to Bebel, Liebknecht, Bracke and others, *ibid.* p.327.
68. Cited in James Joll, *The Second International,* London 1968, p.94.
69. Chris Harman, 'Party and Class', in Duncan Hallas et al, *Party and Class,* London (nd), p.50.
70. Engels to Sorge, 9 August 1890, cited in Monty Johnstone, *op.cit.* p.157.

2. Lenin and the birth of Bolshevism

1. Tony Cliff, 'Trotsky on Substitutionism', in Duncan Hallas et al., *Party and Class,* London (nd), p.28. By 'substitutionism' Cliff means the tendency of individuals or parties to substitute themselves for the action of the masses.
2. Lenin, *What Is To Be Done?* Moscow 1969, p.29.
3. See Leonard Schapiro, *The Communist Party of the Soviet Union,* London 1970, pp.2,5.
4. Lenin, *What Is To Be Done? op.cit.* p.117.
5. *ibid.* p.121.
6. Leonard Schapiro, *op.cit.* p.40.
7. Lenin, *What Is To Be Done? op.cit.* p.121.
8. Lenin, *One Step Forward, Two Steps Back,* Moscow 1969, p.58.
9. Lenin, *Collected Works,* Vol.8, Moscow 1962, p.196.

10.   Lenin, *What Is To Be Done? op.cit.* p.17.

11.   *ibid.* p.17.

12.   This was Plekhanov's statement at the First Congress of the Second International in 1889.

13.   The best exposition of this theory and its socio-economic basis in Russian history is to be found in the first chapter of Trotsky's *The History of the Russian Revolution*, London 1977.

14.   Although economism in fact first arose in 1897. See Lenin, *What Is To Be Done? op.cit.* p.46.

15.   Lenin, *Collected Works*, Vol.4, *op.cit.* p.174.

16.   This does not, however, mean that they can be dragged from their context and applied uncritically in all times and places, thus using the letter of Leninism against the spirit of Leninism as has so often been done.

17.   Cited in Lenin, *What Is To Be Done? op.cit.* p.37.

18.   Lenin, *What Is To Be Done? op.cit.* p.46.

19.   Fatalism carried to its logical conclusion precludes the need for a revolutionary party, or even for any revolutionary activity. The problem with fatalism in the marxist movement, however, is that is has never openly announced itself but has always remained half-developed in such a way as to paralyse revolutionary intervention at crucial moments without exposing its bankruptcy and absurdity.

20.   Lenin, *What Is To Be Done? op.cit.* p.23.

21.   *ibid.* p.131.

22.   Georg Lukacs, *Lenin*, London 1970, p.24.

23.   Lenin, *What Is To Be Done? op.cit.* p.69.

24.   *ibid.* p.78.

25.   *ibid.* p.79.

26.   *ibid.* p.80.

27.   *ibid.* p.88.

28.   *ibid.* p.86. For an excellent account and analysis of this period see Tony Cliff, 'From a Marxist Circle to Agitation', *International Socialism*, 52.

29.   Lenin, *What Is To Be Done? op.cit.* pp.31–32.

30.   *ibid.* p.40.

31.   Trotsky, *Stalin*, London 1968, p.58.

32.   Lucio Magri, 'Problems of the Marxist Theory of the Revolutionary Party', *New Left Review*, 60, p.104.

33.   Nigel Harris, *Beliefs in Society*, London 1971, p.156.

34.   Marx, *Selected Writings on Sociology and Social Philosophy*, in T.B.Bottomore and M.Rubel (eds.), London 1963, pp.80–81.

35.   Raya Dunayevskaya, *Marxism and Freedom*, London 1972, p.81.

36.   Paul Frölich, *Rosa Luxemburg*, London 1972, pp.82–83.

37.   Lenin, *One Step Forward, Two Steps Back, op.cit.* p.66.

38.   Raya Dunayevskaya, *op.cit.* pp.180–81.

39.   Lenin, *One Step Forward, Two Steps Back, op.cit.* p.199.

40. *ibid.* pp.121–23.
41. *ibid.* p.57.
42. *ibid.* p.58.
43. *ibid.* p.71.

3. Lenin: From Russian Bolshevism to the Communist International

1. See Lenin, *Collected Works*, Vol.17, Moscow 1962, pp.74–75.
2. *ibid.* Vol.19, p.301.
3. *ibid.* Vol.19, p.298.
4. Trotsky, *The Permanent Revolution and Results and Prospects*, New York 1969, p.114.
5. The worst offenders in this respect are of course official Soviet historians and theorists for whom Lenin has become an infallible pope, but there is a tendency in this direction even in such works as Lukacs' *Lenin*.
6. Trotsky, 'Hands off Rosa Luxemburg', in Mary Alice Waters (ed.), *Rosa Luxemburg Speaks*, New York 1970, p.444.
7. Lenin's arguments are summed up in *Two Tactics of Social-Democracy in the Democratic Revolution*, Peking 1965.
8. Resolution of the 1905 Menshevik Caucasian Conference, cited in *ibid.* p.102.
9. For Lenin's condemnation of this and his comparison of Plekhanov's attitude to 1905 with Marx's to the Paris Commune, see *Collected Works*, Vol.12, *op.cit.* pp.104–12.
10. Lenin, *Collected Works*, Vol.16, *op.cit.* p.380.
11. Lenin, *Two Tactics of Social-Democracy in the Democratic Revolution*, *op.cit.* pp.2–3.
12. Lenin, *Collected Works*, Vol.10, *op.cit.* p.32.
13. Lenin, *Two Tactics of Social-Democracy in the Democratic Revolution*, *op.cit.* p.155.
14. Lenin, *Collected Works*, Vol.13, *op.cit.* p.108.
15. Lenin, *Two Tactics of Social-Democracy in the Democratic Revolution*, *op.cit.* p.155.
16. *ibid.* p.2.
17. N.Krupskaya, *Memories of Lenin*, London 1970, pp.115–16.
18. Trotsky, *Stalin*, London 1968, pp.64–65.
19. Lenin, *Collected Works*, Vol.10, *op.cit.* p.19.
20. *ibid.* Vol.10, p.19.
21. *ibid.* Vol.10, p.23.
22. *ibid.* Vol.8, p.219.
23. *ibid.* Vol.10, p.36.
24. *ibid.* Vol.10, p.32.
25. *ibid.* Vol.15, p.355.

26.   Lenin summarised the experience of the Bolshevik party, laying special stress on the period of the reaction, as the basis for his arguments against ultra-leftism in *Left Wing Communism–An Infantile Disorder.*

27.   Lenin, *Left Wing Communism–An Infantile Disorder*, Moscow 1960 p.12.

28.   *ibid.* p.13.

29.   See Trotsky, 'Our Differences', in *1905*, New York 1971, pp.299–318.

30.   Because of the censorship Aesopian language had to be employed. Thus the Bolshevik programme was referred to as 'the uncurtailed demands of 1905'.

31.   See Tony Cliff, 'Lenin's *Pravda*', *International Socialism*, 67, p.12.

32.   See Lenin, *Collected Works*, Vol.20, *op.cit.* p.363.

33.   *ibid.* p.366.

34.   D.Lane, *The Roots of Russian Communism*, Assen 1969, p.26.

35.   *ibid.* p.50.

36.   Lenin, *Collected Works*, Vol.20, *op.cit.* p.369.

37.   O.Piatnitsky, *The Bolshevisation of the Communist Parties by Eradicating the Social-Democratic Traditions*, Communist International Publication 1934, printed by London Alliance in Defence of Workers' Rights (nd), p.5.

38.   *ibid.* p.6.

39.   Figures calculated from D.Lane, *op.cit.* p.37.

40.   Trotsky, *The Revolution Betrayed*, London 1967, p.159.

41.   D.Lane, *op.cit.* p.37.

42.   Leonard Schapiro comments: 'It will be recalled that, in the Russian context, the phrase originated in the German Social Democratic Movement, and was first used in 1865 by J.B.Schweitzer, one of the principal followers of Lasalle.' Leonard Schapiro, *The Communist Party of the Soviet Union*, London 1970, p.75 fn.

43.   Lenin, *Collected Works*, Vol.11, *op.cit.* p.320.

44.   *ibid.* pp.320–21.

45.   O.Piatnitsky, *op.cit.* p.13.

46.   Trotsky, *Stalin, op.cit.* p.168.

47.   Lenin, *Collected Works*, Vol.21, *op.cit.* p.16.

48.   *ibid.* p.16.

49.   *ibid.* pp.16–17.

50.   *ibid.* p.17.

51.   *ibid.* p.31.

52.   *ibid.* p.34.

53.   *ibid.* p.93.

54.   *ibid.* p.162.

55.   *ibid.* p.110.

56.   Karl Kautsky, cited in Lenin, *Marxism On the State*, Moscow 1972, p.78.

57.   *ibid.*

58.   Lenin, 'Materialism and Empirio-Criticism', *Collected Works*, Vol. 14, *op.cit.*

59.   Lenin, 'Philosophical Notebooks', *Collected Works*, Vol.38, *op.cit.*

60.   This theme is discussed in greater depth in relation to Gramsci in Chapter 6.

61. See Engels to Marx, 7 October 1858, in Marx and Engels, *Selected Correspondence, op.cit.* p.110, and Engels to Kautsky, 12 September 1882, *ibid.* p.351.

62. Lenin, *Collected Works*, Vol.23, *op.cit.* p.115.

63. *ibid.* p.116.

64. *ibid.* pp.116–17.

65. *ibid.* p.116.

66. Because Lenin wrote *The State and Revolution* in August–September 1917 it is frequently assumed that the inspiration for this theoretical advance came from the experience of the Russian Revolution. In fact Lenin first referred to the need for a theoretical study of the state in response to an article by Bukharin (see Lenin, *Collected Works*, Vol.23, *op.cit.* pp.165–66) and by February 1917 Lenin had completed all the preparations for this. His notebooks have been published as Lenin, *Marxism on the State: Preparatory Material for the Book: 'The State and Revolution'*, Moscow 1972. (For some reason they are not included in the English editions of the *Collected Works*.) An examination of this material shows that it contains all the essential ideas of *The State and Revolution*.

67. Karl Kautsky, *The Road to Power*, Chicago 1910, p.95, cited in Chris Harman, 'Party and Class', London (nd), p.50.

68. Karl Kautsky, *The Erfurt Programme*, Chicago 1910, p.188, cited in *ibid.* p.49.

69. Marx, *The Civil War in France*, Peking 1966, p.64.

70. Lenin, *Marxism on the State: Preparatory Material for the book: 'The State and Revolution'*, *op.cit.* pp.50–51.

71. To say this does not mean that the revolution must necessarily involve a great deal of bloodshed. This will depend on the balance of forces and the reaction of the ruling class. But it does necessarily involve the use of 'illegal' and 'unconstitutional' physical force, precisely because the revolution overthrows the old legality, the old constitution, and the corresponding power structures.

72. Lenin, *The State and Revolution*, Peking 1965, pp.139–40.

73. Chris Harman, 'Party and Class', *op.cit.* p.63.

74. Of course after the revolution in Russia (we shall discuss this question again in relation to the actual seizure of power in October) reality did not at all conform to this schema. At first slowly, and then with increasing speed, party and state began to merge, until before long they were to all intents and purposes identical. But this was not a gradual translation of theory into practice. Rather it was one aspect of the degeneration of the revolution as a whole, produced by the combination of Russia's isolation, its backwardness, the devastation of its economy and the decimation and demoralisation of the Russian working class.

75. The August figure was a guess by Sverdlov, the party secretary. The January and April figures were official party figures but are also only approximations.

76. Leonard Schapiro, *op.cit.* p.173.

77. Martov to Axelrod, 19 November 1917, cited in I.Getzler, *Martov*, Cambridge 1967, p.172.

78. E.H.Carr, Vol.1, p.81.

79. Trotsky, *The History of the Russian Revolution*, London 1977, p.236.

80. Trotsky writes: 'Spartacus Week in January 1919 in Berlin belonged to the same type of intermediate, semi-revolution as the July Days in Petrograd . . . The thing lacking was a Bolshevik party.' *ibid.* p.591.

81. E.H.Carr, Vol.1, *op.cit.* p.109.

82. The decision was taken by 10 votes to 2 on a resolution moved by Lenin on 10 October (i.e. 23 October in the Russian (Julian) Calendar). For the discussion see, *The Bolsheviks and the October Revolution.* Minutes of the Central Committee of the Russian Social-Democratic Labour Party (Bolsheviks) August 1917–February 1918, London 1974, pp.85–89.

83. Thus Leonard Schapiro writes: 'This is the story of how a group of determined men seized power for themselves in Russia in 1917, and kept others from sharing it.' *The Origin of the Communist Autocracy*, London 1966, p.v.

84. Lenin, *Collected Works*, Vol.26, *op.cit.* p.144.

85. *ibid.* Vol.24, p.48.

86. *ibid.* p.49.

87. *ibid.* Vol.25, p.189.

88. *ibid.*

89. *ibid.* Vol. 26, p.303.

90. *ibid.* Vol.24, p.45.

91. *ibid.* p.44.

92. For the arguments of this group see the document by Kamenev and Zinoviev on 'The Current Situation', in *The Bolsheviks and the October Revolution, op.cit.* pp.89–95.

93. See Lenin, *Collected Works*, Vol.26, *op.cit.* p.84.

94. *ibid.* p.282.

95. We refer here, of course, to the early years of the Comintern, specifically to the period of its first four congresses.

96. Jane Degras (ed.), *The Communist International 1919–1943. Documents.* Vol.1, p.164.

97. *ibid.* p.165.

98. Trotsky, *On Lenin*, London 1971, p.143.

99. Georg Lukacs, *op.cit.* p.59.

100. Centrism—the Leninist term for the Kautskyite 'centre' of German Social Democracy and similar trends in other countries e.g. Martov in Russia, Serrati in Italy and MacDonald in England.

101. Lenin, *Collected Works*, Vol.31, *op.cit.* pp.206–207.

102. *ibid.* p.207.

103. *ibid.* p.208.

104. Jane Degras (ed.), *op.cit.* Vol.1, p.167.

105. Lenin, *Collected Works, op.cit.* Vol.31, pp.250–51.

106. For Lenin's speech on the question see *Collected Works*, Vol.31, *op.cit.* p.235–39. For Trotsky's see *The First Five Years of The Communist International*, Vol.1, New York 1973, pp.97–101.

107. Jane Degras (ed.), *op.cit.* Vol.1, p.131.

108. Lenin, *Left Wing Communism—An Infantile Disorder*, *op.cit.* p.25.
109. *ibid.* p.38.
110. *ibid.* p.42.
111. *ibid.* p.38.
112. *ibid.* p.42.
113. Engels, cited *ibid.* p.50.
114. *ibid.* p.52.
115. *ibid.*
116. For a more detailed account of the 'March action' disaster, see Franz Borkenau, *World Communism*, Ann Arbor 1971, pp.214–20.
117. Lenin, *Collected Works*, Vol.32, *op.cit.* p.469.
118. Jane Degras (ed.), Vol.1, *op.cit.* p.243.
119. *ibid.* p.259.
120. For a further discussion of the united front see Chapter 5 below.
121. Lenin, *Collected Works*, Vol.29, *op.cit.* p.310.
122. The fourth congress was quite explicit on this point. A unanimously adopted resolution included the statement: 'The fourth world congress reminds the proletariat of all countries that the proletarian revolution can never triumph completely within a single country, rather it must triumph internationally, as world revolution.' Jane Degras (ed.), Vol.1, *op.cit.* p.444. This question also is taken up more fully in Chapter 5.
123. Lenin, *Collected Works*, Vol.33, *op.cit.* pp.430–32.
124. Trotsky, *The First Five Years of the Communist International*, Vol.1, *op.cit.* p.v.
125. Lenin, *Collected Works*, Vol.22, *op.cit.* p.286.

4. Rosa Luxemburg's alternative view

1. It was Rosa Luxemburg's continued involvement in the Social Democratic Party of the Kingdom of Poland (SDKPL) which explains her particular concern with Russia, since Poland was then part of the Russian Empire.
2. This was published in English under the misleading title of 'Leninism or Marxism?', in Rosa Luxemburg, *The Russian Revolution and Leninism or Marxism?*, edited and introduced by Bertram D. Wolfe, Ann Arbor 1971.
3. *ibid.* pp.82–83.
4. *ibid.* p.83.
5. *ibid.*
6. *ibid.* p.85.
7. *ibid.* p.86.
8. *ibid.* p.88.
9. *ibid.*
10. *ibid.* p.89.
11. *ibid.* p.91.
12. *ibid.* p.94.
13. *ibid.*
14. *ibid.* p.104.

15. *ibid.* p.103.
16. *ibid.*
17. *ibid.* p.108.
18. *ibid.* p.185.
19. *ibid.* p.188.
20. *ibid.* p.69–71.
21. *ibid.* p.85.
22. Rosa Luxemburg, 'The Mass Strike, the Political Party and the Trade Unions', in Mary Alice Waters (ed.), *Rosa Luxemburg Speaks*, New York 1970, pp.207–208.
23. Rosa Luxemburg, 'The Junius Pamphlet', in Mary Alice Waters (ed.), *op.cit.* p.331.
24. Rosa Luxemburg, 'The Mass Strike, the Political Party and the Trade Unions', *op.cit.* p.189.
25. J.P.Nettl, *Rosa Luxemburg*, Vol.1, London 1966, p.265.
26. Bertram D. Wolfe, 'Introduction' to Rosa Luxemburg, *The Russian Revolution and Marxism or Leninism?*, *op.cit.* p.1. This view has some strange and heterogeneous supporters, including Stalinists, for whom any criticism of Lenin was tantamount to heresy and for whom Luxemburg's emphasis on working-class spontaneity represented not only a deviation but also a threat. (For an account of Luxemburg at the hands of Soviet and East European historians see J.P.Nettl, *op.cit.* Vol.II, Chapter XVIII, and Trotsky, 'Hands off Rosa Luxemburg', in Mary Alice Waters (ed.), *op.cit.* pp.441–50); and various anarchists, anarcho-syndicalists, and 'Luxemburgists' who have sought to form groups or movements independent of Stalinism or Trotskyism. (See Trotsky, 'Rosa Luxemburg and the Fourth International', in Mary Alice Waters (ed.), *op.cit.* pp.451–54).
27. This critique of some aspects of Bolshevik policy in the Russian Revolution was written by Luxemburg in prison in 1918, and never published in her lifetime. It did not see the light of day until Paul Levi published it in 1921, when he was expelled from the Communist International.
28. Rosa Luxemburg, *The Russian Revolution and Leninism or Marxism?*, *op.cit.* p.80.
29. Wolfe's contention that Luxemburg opposed the formation of the Third International is, typically, based on the misleading elevation of a tactical disagreement over timing into a matter of principle.
30. Cited in Paul Frölich, *Rosa Luxemburg*, London 1972, p.140.
31. See Rosa Luxemburg, *The Russian Revolution and Leninism or Marxism?*, *op.cit.* p.93.
32. These figures are calculated from the strike statistics in *Sozialgeschichtliches Arbeitsbuch, Materialien zur Statistik des Kaiserreichs 1870–1914*, Munich 1975, p.132.
33. Figures from Trotsky, *The History of the Russian Revolution*, London 1977, p.59.
34. Cited in Tony Cliff, *Rosa Luxemburg*, London 1959, p.52.

35. Duncan Hallas, 'The Way Forward', in John Palmer and Nigel Harris (eds.), *World Crisis*, London 1971, p.266.
36. For a marxist who takes a similar view see Tony Cliff, *Rosa Luxemburg, op.cit.* p.45.
37. It should be noted that when, in 1910, the German working class went into battle for equal suffrage, Luxemburg herself 'demanded that the Party Executive work out a great plan of action'. Paul Frölich, *op.cit.* p.171.
38. See J.P.Nettl, Vol.II, *op.cit.* p.747.
39. *ibid.* p.752.
40. Paul Frölich, *op.cit.* p.279.
41. *ibid.* p.270.
42. J.P.Nettl, *op.cit.* Vol.II, p.724.
43. Cited in Paul Frölich, *op.cit.* p.143.
44. Once we have grasped this fundamental weakness many of Rosa Luxemburg's other errors fall into place—for example her opposition to the right of nations to self-determination and to the Bolshevik policy of land to the peasants. In both these cases it was the uneven development of socialist consciousness among the masses that dictated the tactics of the Bolsheviks and in both cases Luxemburg failed to grasp this.
45. Tony Cliff, *Rosa Luxemburg, op.cit.* p.43.
46. Rosa Luxemburg, 'The Mass Strike, the Political Party and the Trade Unions', *op.cit.* p.202.
47. For extracts from, and a discussion of, this pamphlet, see Paul Frölich *op.cit.* pp.102–108. Unfortunately Frölich makes an unconvincing attempt to equate Luxemburg's views on insurrection with Lenin's.

5. Trotsky's dual legacy

1. For an account of the basic causes of the degeneration of the Russian Revolution see Chris Harman, 'How the Revolution was Lost', *International Socialism*, 30.
2. Trotsky, *The Revolution Betrayed*, London 1967, p.292.
3. Marx and Engels, *The Communist Manifesto, op.cit.* p.76.
4. This rule prohibited party members earning over a certain maximum (approximately equal to the wage of a skilled worker). It was later secretly abolished by Stalin.
5. Trotsky, *The New Course*, Ann Arbor 1965.
6. *ibid.* p.12.
7. *ibid.*
8. *ibid.* p.21.
9. *ibid.* p.25.
10. *ibid.* p.51.
11. *ibid.* p.29.
12. *ibid.* p.28.
13. *ibid.* p.27.

14. Max Shachtman, 'Introduction' to Trotsky, *The New Course, op.cit.* p.3.
15. *The Platform of the Joint Opposition 1927*, London 1973, pp.62–63.
16. *ibid.* p.113.
17. Trotsky, *The Revolution Betrayed, op.cit.* pp.94–95.
18. *ibid.* p.96.
19. *ibid.* p.267.
20. Trotsky, *The Death Agony of Capitalism and the Tasks of the Fourth International*, London 1972, p.51.
21. For Trotsky's critique of international Communist policy (1924–39) see especially *The Third International After Lenin*, New York 1970, *Problems of the Chinese Revolution*, Ann Arbor 1967, *The Struggle Against Fascism in Germany*, New York 1971 and *The Spanish Revolution (1931–39)*, New York 1973.
22. See Trotsky, Introduction to *Terrorism and Communism*, Ann Arbor 1961.
23. Trotsky, *The Struggle Against Fascism in Germany*, New York 1971, p.420.
24. Trotsky, 'Fighting Against the Stream', cited in Duncan Hallas, 'Against the Stream', *International Socialism*, 53 p.36.
25. James P. Cannon, *History of American Trotskyism*, cited in *ibid.* p.32.
26. Zimmerwald was the famous conference at which the internationalist social democrats regrouped themselves in 1915.
27. This tactic was known as the 'French turn' because it began with entry into the French Socialist Party, and was the inspiration for the tactic of entrism practised by many Trotskyist groups in later years.
28. See Trotsky, *In Defence of Marxism*, London 1966, pp.136,140.
29. Cited in Duncan Hallas, 'Against the Stream', *op.cit.*
30. Trotsky, *The Death Agony of Capitalism and the Tasks of the Fourth International*, *op.cit.* pp.12–13.
31. *ibid.* p.43.
32. *ibid.* p.15.
33. Trotsky, *The Revolution Betrayed, op.cit.* p.231.
34. *ibid.* p.227.
35. Trotsky, *The Death Agony of Capitalism and the Tasks of the Fourth International*, *op.cit.* p.43.
36. Trotsky, 'Introduction' to the 1936 French edition of *Terrorism and Communism*; see *Terrorism and Communism*, Ann Arbor 1961, p.xxxv.
37. Trotsky's prediction that the Stalinist regime would collapse in war was based on his view that the Soviet bureaucracy was not a fully fledged social class, but a parasitic caste, without deep roots in Russian society—it was he argued, 'a policeman in the sphere of distribution' (see *The Revolution Betrayed, op.cit.* p.112) not a—'ruling class indispensable to the given system of economy' (see *In Defence of Marxism, op.cit.* p.29). This characterisation followed from Trotsky's analysis of the Soviet Union as a degenerated workers' state. That the Stalinist bureaucracy demonstrated a totally unexpected stability and durability is one piece of evidence that Trotsky's analysis was incorrect and that the bureaucracy is indeed a social class presiding over a state capitalist

economic system. (See Tony Cliff, *State Capitalism in Russia*, London 1974, especially pp.166–68, and pp.275–77.

38. Cited in Duncan Hallas, 'Against the Stream', *op.cit.* p.37.
39. The Mezhrayontsy, or inter-borough organisation, had a somewhat larger membership in Petrograd alone than did most of the national sections of the Fourth International, yet in 1917 no-one doubted that it was too small to really influence events. Only by merging his organisation with the Bolsheviks was Trotsky able to participate effectively in the shaping of history.
40. Trotsky, *The Death Agony of Capitalism and the Tasks of the Fourth International*, *op.cit.* pp.14–15.
41. Trotsky, *The Third International After Lenin*, New York 1970, p.140.
42. Trotsky, *The Death Agony of Capitalism and the Tasks of the Fourth International*, *op.cit.* p.58.
43. James P. Canon, *The Militant*, 17 November 1945, cited in Duncan Hallas 'The Fourth International in Decline', *International Socialism*, 60, p.17.
44. Cited in *ibid.* p.19.
45. One who did take this step was Trotsky's wife Natalia Sedova. Resigning from the Fourth International in 1951 she wrote:

Obsessed by old and outlived formulas, you continue to regard the Stalinist state as a workers' state. I cannot and will not follow you in this . . . Virtually every year after the beginning of the fight against the usurping Stalinist bureaucracy, L. D. Trotsky repeated that the regime was moving to the right . . . if this trend continues, he said, the revolution will be at an end and the restoration of capitalism will be achieved . . . That, unfortunately, is what has happened even if in new and unexpected forms . . . you now hold that the states of Eastern Europe over which Stalinism established its domination during and after the war, are likewise workers' states. This is equivalent to saying that Stalinism has carried out a revolutionary socialist role. I cannot and will not follow you in this. (*Natalia Trotsky and the Fourth International*, London 1972, pp.9–10).

Another was Tony Cliff, who, in 1947, produced the first fully worked out analysis of state capitalism in Russia (See *State Capitalism in Russia, op.cit.).*

6. Gramsci's Modern Prince

1. To deceive the prison censor Gramsci avoided all use of conventional marxist terminology, and all direct mention of well known revolutionaries. Thus 'class' is rendered 'fundamental social group'; 'oppressed class' is 'subaltern group'; Trotsky is Lev Davidovitch; Lenin is Ilych, or 'the recent great theoretician'; and marxism is 'the philosophy of praxis'.
2. Antonio Gramsci, *Selections from the Prison Notebooks*, London 1971, p.387.
3. *ibid.* p.465.
4. *ibid.* p.336.
5. *ibid.* pp.336–37.
6. *ibid.* p.438.

7. *ibid.* p.407.
8. *ibid.* p.160.
9. *ibid.*
10. *ibid.* p.233.
11. *ibid.* p.104.
12. *ibid.* pp.180–81.
13. *ibid.* p.183.
14. *ibid.* p.325.
15. *ibid.* p.323.
16. See *ibid.* p.192.
17. To illustrate this point we have the example of Lukacs who similarly approached the question of the party on the basis of a critique of mechanical materialism, but who remained entirely within the terrain of philosophy. Lukacs conceived of the party as the bearer and embodiment of proletarian class consciousness, but because he defined class consciousness in an unhistorical and rationalistic way he fell into an idealised and elitist view of the party which failed to add anything useful to, indeed fell short of, Lenin.
18. Cited in John Merrington, 'Theory and practice in Gramsci's marxism', *Socialist Register*, 1968, p.165.
19. Antonio Gramsci, *Soviets in Italy*, London 1969, pp.22–23.
20. Published in *Soviets in Italy, op.cit.*
21. *ibid.* p.35.
22. Antonio Gramsci, *Selections from the Prison Notebooks, op.cit.* p.123.
23. *ibid.* p.129.
24. For the background to this see *ibid.* p.169.
25. *ibid.* pp.169–70.
26. *ibid.* p.124.
27. *ibid.* p.238.
28. *ibid.* p.235.
29. *ibid.* pp.229–39.
30. *ibid.* p.120.
31. *ibid.* p.239.
32. *ibid.* p.238.
33. Antonio Gramsci, 'The Southern Question', in *The Modern Prince and Other Writings*, New York 1972, pp.30–31.
34. Antonio Gramsci, *Selections from the Prison Notebooks, op.cit.* p.168.
35. *ibid.*
36. Gramsci's brother Gennaro visited him in prison to ascertain his attitude to the 'third period' but, on finding that he opposed it, kept the information secret in case his brother should be expelled. See Giuseppe Fiori, *Antonio Gramsci: Life of a Revolutionary*, London 1970, pp.252–53.
37. Antonio Gramsci, *Selections from the Prison Notebooks, op.cit.* p.185.
38. *ibid.* p.340.

39. Gramsci makes this point as part of an analysis of Italian political parties 'in general' but, as so often with Gramsci's 'abstract' discussions, there is a clear implication for the practice of the revolutionary party.
40. Antonio Gramsci, *Selections from the Prison Notebooks, op.cit.* p.227.
41. For Gramsci's analysis of 'the intellectuals' see *ibid.* pp.5–23.
42. *ibid.* p.340.
43. Antonio Gramsci, *The Modern Prince and Other Writings, op.cit.* pp.50–51.
44. Antonio Gramsci, *Selections from the Prison Notebooks, op.cit.* pp.196–97.
45. *ibid.* p.197.
46. *ibid.* p.199.
47. *ibid.* p.198.
48. *ibid.* pp.198–99.
49. *ibid.* p.199.
50. *ibid.* p.155.
51. *ibid.*
52. *ibid.* p.144.
53. *ibid.* pp.152–53.
54. *ibid.*
55. *ibid.* p.144.
56. Cited in A.Pozzolini, *Antonio Gramsci: An Introduction to his Thought*, London 1970, p.65.
57. Antonio Gramsci, *Selections from the Prison Notebooks, op.cit.* p.188.
58. *ibid.* p.211.
59. *ibid.*
60. *ibid.* p.195.
61. See Antonio Gramsci, *Selections from the Prison Notebooks, op.cit.* pp.236–38. Gramsci records that Trotsky began 'a revision of current tactical methods', along these lines at the fourth congress of the Comintern. But paradoxically, and for reasons that can only be the subject of speculation, he accuses Trotsky of being: 'the political theorist of frontal attack in a period which leads only to defeats'. (*ibid.* p.238.)
62. Antonio Gramsci, *Selections from the Prison Notebooks, op.cit.* p.173.
63. *ibid.* p.liii.

7. The revolutionary party today

1. As Che Guevara put it when summing up the essence of guerilla warfare:
   1. Popular forces can win a war against the army.
   2. It is not necessary to wait until all conditions for making revolution exist; the insurrection can create them.
   3. In underdeveloped America the countryside is the basic area for armed fighting. (*Guerilla Warfare*, New York 1961, p.15.)
2. The Cuban situation was exceptional in two respects: (a) the Batista regime was in a state of advanced dissolution and decay and gave up almost without a fight; (b) the United States believed they could use the rebels to serve their

own purposes and were not initially hostile—an error they did not repeat. Also, speaking of 'success in Cuba' should not be taken to mean success of the socialist revolution. The Cuban revolutionaries themselves did not claim as much at the time. Only after Cuba had opted for the Communist bloc in 1961 did the Cuban revolution become retrospectively 'socialist'. In fact the absence of a successful struggle for *self*-emancipation by the working class meant that the economic structure of Cuba necessarily became state capitalist.

3.   See Frank Roberts, 'The Tupamaros', *International Socialism*, 65.

4.   See Tony Cliff and Ian Birchall, *France: The Struggle Goes On*, London 1968.

5.   For an analysis and critique of the strategy of Popular Unity by a participant in the events, see Helios Prieto, *Chile: The Gorillas are Amongst Us*, London 1974.

6.   For example: Lucio Magri, 'Problems of the Marxist Theory of the Revolutionary Party', *New Left Review*, 60; Rossana Rossanda, 'Class and Party', *Socialist Register*, 1970; Jean-Paul Sartre, 'Masses, Spontaneity, Party', *Socialist Register*, 1970; Ernest Mandel, 'The Leninist Theory of Organisation', London (nd); Monty Johnstone, 'Marx and Engels and the Concept of the Party', *Socialist Register*, 1967; Chris Harman, 'Party and Class' and Tony Cliff, 'Trotsky on "Substitutionism"', in Duncan Hallas et al, *Party and Class*, London, (nd).

Index

About Haymarket Books

Haymarket Books is a radical, independent, nonprofit book publisher based in Chicago.

Our mission is to publish books, particularly new and classical works of Marxism, that contribute to struggles for social and economic justice. We strive to make our books a vibrant and organic part of social movements and the education and development of a critical, engaged, international left.

We take inspiration and courage from our namesakes, the Haymarket martyrs, who gave their lives fighting for a better world. Their 1886 struggle for the eight-hour day—which gave us May Day, the international workers' holiday—reminds workers around the world that ordinary people can organize and struggle for their own liberation. These struggles continue today across the globe—struggles against oppression, exploitation, poverty, and war.

Since our founding in 2001, Haymarket Books has published more than five hundred titles. Radically independent, we seek to drive a wedge into the risk-averse world of corporate book publishing. Our authors include Eqbal Ahmad, Arundhati Roy, Angela Y. Davis, Howard Zinn, Ian Birchall, Ahmed Shawki, Paul Le Blanc, Mike Davis, Kim Scipes, Ilan Pappé, Michael Roberts, Sharon Smith, Dave Zirin, Keeanga-Yamahtta Taylor, Nick Turse, Kim Moody, Danny Katch, Jeffery R. Webber, Paul D'Amato, Amira Hass, Sherry Wolf, Naomi Klein, and Neil Davidson. We are also the trade publishers of the acclaimed Historical Materialism Book Series, and of the Studies in Critical Social Sciences book series, as well as Dispatch Books.

Shop our full catalog online at www.haymarketbooks.org.

John Molyneux is a socialist, activist and writer. His books include *What is the Real Marxist Tradition?* and *The Future Socialist Society*. He formerly lectured at Portsmouth University and now lives in Dublin. He is editor of the *Irish Marxist Review*.